To the middle school ministry of Journey Community Church in La Mesa, California. You've given me a place to belong as a former junior high pastor who still has a strong passion for and calling to young teens.

Mark Oestreicher

DARES FROM JESUS

12 Wild Lessons
with Truth and Dares
for junior highers

Wild Truth Bible Lessons

ZONDERVAN®

ZONDERVAN.com/
AUTHORTRACKER
follow your favorite authors

Youth Specialties
.com

Youth Specialties

Wild Truth Bible Lessons—Dares from Jesus: 12 wild lessons with truth and dares for junior highers
Copyright © 2002 by Youth Specialties

Youth Specialties products, 300 S. Pierce St., El Cajon, CA 92020, are published by Zondervan, 5300 Patterson Ave. S.E., Grand Rapids, MI 49530.

Library of Congress Cataloging-In-Publication Data

Oestreicher, Mark.
    Wild truth Bible lessons—dares from Jesus : 12 wild lessons with truth and dares for junior highers / Mark Oestreicher.
       p. cm.
    ISBN-10: 0-310-24187-1
    ISBN-13: 978-0-310-24187-4
    1. Christian Eduacation of teenagers 2. Jesus Christ—person and offices—Biblical teaching. I. Title:Dares from Jesus. II. Title.

    BV4447 .O473 2002
    268'.433—dc21

                                2002005473

Edited by Rick Marschall and Linda Bannan
Illustrations by Krieg Barrie
Design by Tom Gulotta
Production assistance by Sarah Sheerin

Printed in the United States of America

---

11 • 15 14 13 12

Contents

Acknowledgments

Thanks to the El Cajon Coffee Company, whose back porch provided moments of concentration while writing this book. Thanks to Todd Temple—the Wild Truth flamefanner—for the *Dares From Jesus* concept. Thanks to Rick Marschall and the other YS product team staffers for your patience on this horrendously late manuscript. And, as always, thanks to my love, Jeannie, and my two little loves, Liesl and Max, for your non stop, surprising charity and acceptance.

Come on—admit it.

When you were a teenager, you played Truth or Dare. At some point. *You probably played spin-the-bottle too—but that's a subject for a different book.*

The best games of Truth or Dare, when we were teens, were those played with creative people who came up with great truths and killer dares. You never knew which one to choose, because it was clear they would be equally challenging.

Well, Jesus has "plussed" that game. He says to us—and to the junior highers we work with—"Look, I want to play Truth *and* Dare, not Truth *or* Dare!" Jesus is going for the double zinger! Truth *and* Dare! All over the gospels we see Jesus teaching or challenging this way. First he lays out a truth. Then there's an implicit or explicit dare issue: "C'mon—don't be a wimp!"

In *Wild Truth Journal: Dares From Jesus*, I developed 50 Truth and Dare challenges from Jesus for young teens to use on their own or in the context of a small group. This book, *Wild Truth Bible Lessons: Dares From Jesus*, takes 12 of those challenges and expands them into full youth group sessions—active teaching times designed especially with young teens in mind.

There's another book of these babies: *Wild Truth Bible Lessons: Dare From Jesus 2*, if you want to continue this study with your teens. And if you're not familiar with the *Wild Truth* line, there are two preceding sets:

- *Wild Truth Journal; Wild Truth Bible Lessons;* and *Wild Truth Bible Lessons 2*. Each of these focus on life lessons learned from Bible characters.

- *Wild Truth Journal—Pictures of God; Wild Truth Bible Lessons—Pictures of God;* and *Wild Truth Bible Lessons—Pictures of God 2*. Each of these focus on different characteristics (self-portraits from Scripture) of God, and they turn the corner to how we can develop these characteristics in ourselves.

One word of caution about teaching the *Dares From Jesus*: it's dangerously easy to slip into legalism while issuing these challenges. Jesus didn't do this when he issued these dares. Some in the modern church have perfected jumping on any behavioral challenge as an opportunity to fight over legalism.
So be careful.

Each lesson has four sections. Here's what I've tried to do with them:

- *Wanna Play?* is the "hook" (if I may rip off the Christian Education guru Larry Richards). It's designed to bring the group together and get students interested in the subject.

- *It's the Truth* is the "book," in Richards' terminology. It presents the biblical truth—in this case, the truth Jesus is referring to.

- *Truth in Action* is the Richardsian "look"—what does the Bible mean in the life of a young teen? This is a crucial step for young teens, to help them cross the bridge of somewhat abstract biblical concepts to the concrete world of their everyday lives. This section is usually full of case studies, "what if?" scenarios, and speculation exercises.

- *Take the Dare* is the piece Larry would call "took." It's the application— "how am I doing to apply this truth to my life?" I try hard to get kids to make a commitment to a tangible act of application each week—a gusty act, of sorts. It's always best if you're able to follow up on these commitments throughout the week, or the following week when you gather again.

Here's the deal: I absolutely adore junior highers. I'd rather work with young teens than older teens any day of the week! They're open. They're moldable. They don't wear as many masks. I've often felt high school ministry these days is "corrective ministry," while junior high ministry is still "preventive ministry." This is often a far cry from when you and I were young teens.

And I believe with all my heart that those who work with young teens (that would be you!) are some of the most valuable yet under-appreciated wackos in the church. Your ministry to young teens is absolutely critical to the kingdom of God. My hope and prayer is that these lessons won't just be valuable for your students (I certainly want that). But I hope you feel affirmed in your calling as a young teen youth worker as you read through and teach these lessons. I hope you hear the quiet voice of God whispering to you his love and calling and affirmation.

God's richest blessing on you and your kids!

Mark Oestreicher

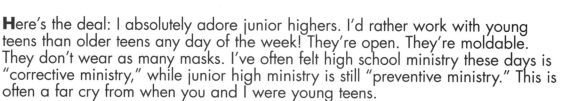

Get Past It!

"You have heard that it was said to the people long ago, 'Do not murder, and anyone who murders will be subject to judgment.' But I tell you that anyone who is angry with his brother will be subject to judgment. Again, anyone who says to his brother, 'Raca,' is answerable to the Sanhedrin. But anyone who says, 'You fool!' will be in danger of the fire of hell.

"Therefore, if you are offering your gift at the altar and there remember that your brother has something against you, leave your gift there in front of the altar. First go and be reconciled to your brother; then come and offer your gift.

"Settle matters quickly with your adversary who is taking you to court. Do it while you are still with him on the way, or he may hand you over to the judge, and the judge may hand you over to the officer, and you may be thrown into prison. I tell you the truth, you will not get out until you have paid the last penny."

Matthew 5:21-26

GOALS

Students Will—

- Understand the biblical concept of reconciliation
- Discuss why God cares about reconciliation, and what it looks like in the lives of young teens
- Choose a personal plan of reconciliation

DESTROY AND REPAIR

You'll Need

- a magazine ad (or a poster), scissors, and a roll of clear tape for each team
- Optional: a small candy prize for the winning team

Divide your students into teams. I'll probably explain this over and over in this book: *you decide the size of the teams, based on the overall size of your group.* I won't treat you like an idiot in this book but as a peer who will tweak and modify what I write here, even if I don't tell you to do so! So if you have a tiny group (4-7 kids), don't even break up into two teams for this exercise—it will work fine. Otherwise, your teams can be anywhere from 3-4 kids each to 10 kids each. The larger the team, the more helpful it will be to have an adult leader in each team.

Give each team a magazine ad, or better yet, a poster (in other words, something graphic that's not too small). Also give them a pair of scissors. Don't give them the tape yet (or even let them see it)—you don't want them to know that they'll be repairing the damage you'll ask them to do.

Now tell them to destroy their ads or posters. Give them about two minutes to cut or tear or otherwise mutilate the original. If your kids are normal junior highers, this will be a fairly quick process—especially for teams that are predominantly boys. Destruction is part of the DNA of a junior higher!

After all the teams are done with their destructive work, pass out a role of cellophane tape to each group. Tell them they'll have 2 minutes to get the ad or poster back together. Then say, "go!" Some may whine and complain that you hadn't told them they'd be putting the pictures back together. Give them your best "tough luck" grin, and mention that their time is running out.

Modify the two-minute time limit. In other words, if no group is even close to completing their reconstructive work after two minutes, give them a bit more time. You can either declare the first team finished to be the winners, or you can wait until most are done and judge the winners as the best reconstructed original. Consider awarding a small candy prize to the winning team.

THE HUG FEST

Make a transition out of the opening activity by saying something like: **Just like you put those pictures back together—God really cares about a big word called "reconciliation," which means to put relationships back together.**

Now ask for volunteers to participate in a Spontaneous Melodrama (or recruit them before your group meets). They won't have to learn any parts or lines. They just have to be willing to ham it up and act out the drama as you read it. Instruct the actors that when they do have spoken lines, you'll read them, and they should just repeat the lines in character. The characters are:

- **Joe**
- **Jake**
- **Joe's friends** (2-3 actors)
- **The Preacher**

One caution: you should try to recruit a fairly secure student for the role of Jake, since he's such a weird kid. If you recruit an outcast for this role, it could turn into a situation where kids are laughing *at* him rather than *with* him—and that's generally considered a no-no in effective ministry! If you have doubts that any kid in your group could handle the part, recruit a mature high school student or adult leader to play the part.

You'll also want to be ready for the second scene by having two empty seats out in the "audience" (your group) for Jake and Joe to sit in.

Now read the script, pausing for the actors to play their parts. After you read the scripted line of a character, pause for the character to repeat the line. Coach or direct a bit when necessary, encouraging the actors to get into their parts.

After the Melodrama is over, give the actors a big round of applause, then have everyone turn in their Bibles to the dare from Jesus (or display the passage in a way that everyone can see it). I'd discourage you

You'll Need

- volunteer actors for the **Spontaneous Melodrama**, and a copy of the script (at the end of this lesson) for you or another adult leader to read. You'll also need Bibles or some other way to show the scripture passage to your group (PowerPoint or MediaShout).

from simply reading the passage without letting your group *see* it. Junior highers are greatly helped by *seeing* scripture—it helps focus their attention (at least a tiny bit!), and it helps them grasp the passage more.

Read Matthew 5:21-26. Then ask these questions:

- **What's the dare from Jesus?** *Seek reconciliation with others. Try to repair relationships you've damaged. And don't wait to do it!*

- **Why do you think Jesus cares about us repairing hurt relationships?** *It's one of God's biggest goals—to help us experience healthy relationships. It's also one of the ways we show the world we're different—by how we love each other.*

- **Can you think of an ultimate example of reconciliation that Jesus provided for us?** *When Jesus died on the cross, he opened the way for us to be reconciled with God!*

- **Why do you think Jesus wants us to get to this right away—not to wait?** *When we put stuff off, it's easy for it to never get done!*

- **Why is it so difficult to reconcile with people we've wronged?** *They might not want reconciliation. Peoples' pride gets in the way. It's easy to justify the wrong we do to others as paying them back for something they did to us. We don't see many people doing it!*

RECONCILERS, INC.

Have kids work individually or in pairs to fill out the "Job Application" on the **Reconcilers, Inc.** Wildpage (1.1). It's simply a set of three case studies where your students will think through what reconciliation looks like in the life of a young teen.

After kids have had about five minutes to work through the sheet, debrief it by walking

You'll Need

- copies of Wildpage 1.1, on page 15 (Reconcilers, Inc.) and pens or pencils for each student.

through each scenario and asking for possible solutions.

Non paper option: Duh, this would be a great small group discussion without giving out copies of the Wildpage.

DO I DARE?

You'll need something for students to write on. If you used Wildpage 1.1 **(Reconcilers, Inc.)** for the last exercise, you can just have students turn it over and write on the blank backside. If you didn't use the Wildpage, or if you are just a freak about handing out lots and lots of papers to your students (yup, that's me too), make copies of the "Do I Dare?" bookmark page at the end of this lesson and cut them into strips.

Walk your group through four questions:
- **Who have I done harm to?**
- **How did I do harm?**
- **What can I do to reconcile with this person?**
- **Do I Dare?**

Ask the questions one at a time (have your kids write them down if you're using blank paper), and have them write an answer. Talk about each question and different responses kids have before moving on to the next question. Some of your students might have a difficult time thinking of someone they've harmed. If this is the case, ask the group to brainstorm different ways junior highers tend to harm each other. These could include, but are *certainly* not limited to:
- **Physical harm**
- **Gossip**
- **Rumors**
- **Saying mean things**
- **Intimidation**
- **Bullying**
- **Ignoring**
- **Degrading or Teasing**
- **Judging**
- **Creating foul smells around each other**
- **Many, many more ways!**

The last question—"Do I Dare?"—is the challenge. It's asking the students if they're willing to take the dare and try to reconcile with the persons they've just described. If their answer is "no," they should simply write so. Berate them and call them "wimps" (I'm kidding). If their answer is "yes," they should write a time and place for carrying out this reconciliation work.

Be sure to close your time in prayer, thanking God for his ultimate reconciliation work with us of having Jesus die on the cross (and that was reconciliation offered for something *we* had done, not something *He* did!). Also ask for courage to carry out these reconciliation action plans. ʊ̈

The Hug-Fest

Characters:
Joe • Jake • Joe's friends (2-3 actors) • The Preacher

Scene 1

One day Jake was standing in the hallway at school, and he had an urge to spin. Yes, this was strange behavior, but Jake didn't care. He just began to spin around in place. He spun and spun and spun. Eventually, he got really dizzy—he stumbled around trying to get his balance, but fell down to the ground. Then he got up and started spinning again.

Just then, Joe and his friends walked by. Joe and Jake went to the same church and youth group, but they weren't friends or anything. In fact, Joe normally stayed away from Jake because of Jake's weird spinning thing! Joe said to his friends, "Hey, let's teach this weirdo a lesson!"

Joe and his friends surrounded Jake, who was still spinning around. In fact, Jake now had his hands up in the air while he spun around, and was making little "wheee" sounds like a kid on a ride. Joe reached out his hand and stopped Jake. Jake was a little disoriented and off-balance, and he fell down again, taking Joe with him. Joe's friends started laughing uncontrollably.

Joe scrambled back up to his feet and yelled, "Jake, you are so weird!"

Jake smiled, and said, "So what?" Then Jake stood to his feet also.

Joe and his friends started pushing Jake around. They pushed him across their little circle to each other. This went on and on, and eventually, Jake put his hands in the air and started making the "wheee" sound again with a big smile on his face! This made Joe even more frustrated. He threw his knee into Jake's stomach and did an elbow drop on Jake's shoulder, dropping him to the ground again. Then Joe and his friends walked away, leaving Jake on the ground.

Scene 2

That Sunday, Jake and Joe were both sitting in church—not together, of course. Joe was feeling awful about what he'd done to Jake. He just couldn't get it out of his mind. In fact, he'd made up his mind to apologize to Jake at some point—but he had no idea when and where he would do it. This was really bugging him and causing him to twitch and spaz almost uncontrollably.

The preacher was up in front, beginning his sermon. Joe was still twitching and spazzing. Jake was listening and smiling really big. The preacher was really getting into it—banging the pulpit and jumping around. Then he stopped and read the scripture for the morning, which said something like this:

> Therefore, if you are offering your gift at the altar and there remember that your brother has something against you, leave your gift there in front of the altar. First go and be reconciled to your brother; then come and offer your gift.

The scripture hit Joe like a ton of bricks—so much so that he jerked his chair back and fell onto the floor! He knew exactly what he had to do. He stood up and walked straight over to Jake. The preacher was still jumping around and banging the pulpit.

Joe knelt on the ground next to Jake and said, "Bro, what I did to you was totally wrong. Can you forgive me?"

Jake smiled and said, "Okay." Then Joe and Jake gave each other a big hug. And then they both hugged the preacher. And then Joe's friends came running in yelling, "We want hugs too!" And the whole room broke out into a giant hug-fest!

W I L D P A G E

Reconcilers, Inc.

Re: Job Application

Allow us to introduce ourselves: we are Reconcilers, Incorporated. We're a group of young teens who've formed this new partnership to help advise people on how to go about reconciling with someone they've hurt. And we understand that you are interested in a position with our firm. The following application will help us decide if you are a fit for us.

Scenario #1: Jenni's Jealousy

Jenni's friend Maura just made the cheerleading squad, and Jenni didn't. Maura's so excited about it she can't seem to stop talking about the squad and the practices and the cute little uniforms. Jenni is burning up with jealousy and stops talking to Maura. In fact, she doesn't speak with Maura for almost two months! Jenni wants to make things right with Maura. As an employee of Reconcilers, Inc., what would you suggest to her?

Scenario #2: Mike's Mouth

Mike can't shut up! He blabs about everything anyone tells him. And when Carson shares some really personal and confidential stuff about his parents, Mike makes sure everyone in the youth group knows all about it. Carson is really hurt and embarrassed. Mike feels terrible about what he's done. As an employee of Reconcilers, Inc., what would you suggest to him?

Scenario #3: Ryan's Rumor

Ryan's not even sure why he did it. Maybe it was because he was trying to impress people. Whatever the reason, the damage was done now. Ryan made up a rumor about Grace. He'd told people she'd had sex with a couple guys he knows. And everyone believed him! Ryan doesn't think there's any way he can repair the damage he's done without everyone hating him. As an employee of Reconcilers, Inc., what would you suggest to him?

Do I Dare?

Do I Dare?

Who have I done
harm to?

How did I do
harm?

What can I do to
reconcile with
this person?

Do I Dare?

Do I Dare?

Do I Dare?

Who have I done
harm to?

How did I do
harm?

What can I do to
reconcile with
this person?

Do I Dare?

Do I Dare?

Do I Dare?

Who have I done
harm to?

How did I do
harm?

What can I do to
reconcile with
this person?

Do I Dare?

Do I Dare?

Who have I done
harm to?

How did I do
harm?

What can I do to
reconcile with
this person?

Do I Dare?

16

Take Them In Pairs

"You have heard that it was said, 'Eye for eye, and tooth for tooth.' But I tell you, Do not resist an evil person. If someone strikes you on the right cheek, turn to him the other also. And if someone wants to sue you and take your tunic, let him have your cloak as well. If someone forces you to go one mile, go with him two miles. Give to the one who asks you, and do not turn away from the one who wants to borrow from you."

Matthew 5:38-42

GOALS

STUDENTS WILL—

- Understand that the desire to take revenge is a normal, human response that's been around since biblical times
- See how revenge can make a situation worse, leading to tough consequences for everyone involved
- Think about some better, God-pleasing ways to respond instead of striking back when they feel attacked

WANNA PLAY?

CLEARING THE AIR

Begin the lesson by telling your students that something's really been bugging you, and you'd like to tell them about it. Then describe a situation when you were really bothered or hurt by someone. Include lots of details about what happened and how you felt before telling them how you handled

You'll Need

☺ whatever stuff you use to create a list that the whole group can see

the situation (the worse you handled it, the better the illustration for this lesson!).

Ask the kids to raise their hands if they can relate to your story. Now on a white board or similar item used for long-distance viewing, make two numbered columns. Above column one write "Situation." Above column two write "Response."

Ask students to share similar stories with the group. Make up a one or two-word title for each story, and write it in column one. And write a one- or two-word summary of how the storyteller responded in column two. If you have a hard time finding volunteers for this exercise, ask students to share their thoughts in more general terms. Ask them

to name some things or situations that make them hurt, angry, irritated, and so on, and write these examples down in the first column. Ask for possible responses to each bothersome situation and list these in column two.

Briefly discuss the items in both columns. Ask students questions like—

- **Which responses seem fair, given the circumstances?**
- **Which are more extreme or over the top?**
- **Do any of these responses in column two appear to be acts of revenge?**
- **When is it okay to seek revenge on someone?**

Optional Idea:
Revenge, Hollywood Style!

Consider showing a short clip from the junior-high-ministry-approved video *The Princess Bride* (really, I've watched this with junior highers dozens of times over the years – anytime I stood in the video store trying to rent something "appropriate" and couldn't find anything!). Start the tape at 00:17:25 (from the Nelson Entertainment logo, not from the beginning of the tape if you're using video) at about the time when Inigo Montoya says, "Hello there!" to the Dread Pirate Roberts who's climbing up a steep cliff.

In this scene Inigo tells his opponent the story of how he's spent 20 years pursuing the six-fingered man who killed his father.

You'll Need

ᐱ a copy of the 1987 movie *The Princess Bride*

ᐱ or, a copy of the 1998 version of Walt Disney's *The Parent Trap*

Meanwhile, he does some freelance work for a bad guy to "pay the bills" because there's no money in revenge. Depending on your time constraints, you can either end the clip just before they begin to fight, or wait until their sword fight is finished and the Dread Pirate Roberts says, "Please understand I hold you in the highest respect" (00:24:58). The swordplay in this scene could also serve as an illustration of how things escalate, as each man gets more daring and their fight patterns become flashier throughout the fight.

After showing this clip you could ask—

• **What would it feel like to pursue someone for 20 years and not find him or her?**

• **Do you think Inigo was justified in his desire to take the six-fingered man's life as payback for the death of his father? Explain why or why not.**

• **How did the swordplay between these two men resemble typical acts of revenge?** *(They kept trying to outdo each other; each time one of them got the upper hand, they acted just a little more confident or cocky about their abilities; it wasn't until the very end that Inigo finally acted like or admitted that he might not win the fight—he didn't give up easily.)*

• **How did this scene differ from what you think of when you imagine someone getting revenge?** *(Dread Pirate Roberts could have killed Inigo, but he was merciful; they were very courteous and gentlemanly toward each other during the sword fight; they understood why they were fighting each other.)*

Or, if you want to use a more girlie bit, show a scene from the 1998 Disney version of *The Parent Trap*. Start the scene at 00:09:45 (from the Walt Disney logo). The scene begins with two kids fencing and ends after a full-scale cabin raid goes very wrong, and the camp director says, "The isolation cabin!" (00:20:37).

Video Clip Note: If this clip is too long for the time you have to work with, you can start or end the video at a couple of other spots and still get your point across. You could begin the clip at 00:13:31 (a poker game scene) or 00:15:48 (three girls returning to their cabin), and you could end the scene at 00:18:17 (Hayley says, "Thank you very much!") or 00:19:57 (camp director says, "Pack your bags!").

No matter what portion of this video clip you choose to show your kids, be sure you preview it beforehand to make sure you're completely comfortable with what it portrays. At the end of the poker game scene, one of the girls must jump into the lake—buck-naked. They don't show anything but her bare shoulders, but if you teach junior highers First Church of Overreaction, then start the clip at the third suggested start time. Far be it from me to get you in trouble (hee-hee)!

After the clip ask—

• **What could Hayley or Annie have done to end their disagreement sooner?**

• **What circumstances may have prevented the girls from working out their differences peacefully and rationally?**

• **What are some possible negative outcomes that could have resulted from their little games?**

• **Do you think the consequence fit the crime? How would you have handled the situation if you were the camp director?**

REVENGE OF BIBLICAL PROPORTIONS

Tell your students that revenge has been around since the beginning of time. While revenge seeking may seem perfectly justified at the time, these typically violent acts usually bring about dire consequences for both the perpetrator and the recipient.

Summarize the story of Simeon and Levi's terrible plan of attack against an entire village to avenge the rape of their sister (Genesis 34). Your students probably haven't heard this story before, but it's a great illustration of how revenge — even when it seems justified—can get way out of hand. (See below)

copies of **Our Way or His Way?** Wildpage 2.1 (p. 22), pencils or pens for all, and Bibles

Just in case you aren't familiar with the story, Jacob and Leah's only daughter Dinah was raped by a man named Shechem (nice name, huh? It sounds like the noise you make when coughing up phlegm!). After he did this terrible thing, he decided to make good by offering to take Dinah as his wife and let the rest of Jacob's clan intermarry with his. When Dinah's brothers heard what Shechem (excuse me!) did, they were outraged that the man thought he could just smooth things over with a quick marriage proposal. So two of them, Simeon and Levi, came up with a plan of revenge.

First they promised Shechem (pass a tissue, please) and his father Hamor that if every guy in their city would agree to be circumcised, then Shechem (I must have a chest cold) could marry their sister Dinah. The Bible doesn't say so, but Shechem (one last phlegm-wad) and Hamor must have been pretty persuasive fellows because all the men agreed. But that wasn't good enough for Simeon and Levi.

After Shechem's men voluntarily underwent this incredibly painful medical procedure, Simeon and Levi strolled into town and killed every last one of them while they were still recovering in their beds. But even *that* wasn't good enough for the brothers.

So then they looted the city, taking all the women, children, livestock, and other valuables for themselves. In the end their retaliation for Dinah's rape (Shechem's sin) escalated and led Simeon and Levi to commit even more sins against man (and against God) than Shechem did in the first place: lying, killing, and robbing. And all of it was done in the name of defending their sister's honor.

Jacob was horrified by his sons' behavior. He told Simeon and Levi in no uncertain terms that their actions would probably lead to the downfall of the entire family if the rest of their neighbors got wind of what they did. They might just band together against Jacob's clan and destroy them all!

While on his deathbed many years later, Jacob cursed them both, saying, "Simeon and Levi are brothers—their swords are weapons of violence. Let me not enter their council, let me not join their assembly, for they have killed men in their anger and hamstrung oxen as they pleased. Cursed be their anger, so fierce, and their fury, so cruel! I will scatter them in Jacob and disperse them in Israel" (Genesis 49:5-7). And it happened just like he said. The descendants of Simeon and Levi were scattered after Joshua led the Israelites into the Promised Land of Canaan. When the lots were cast to determine how much land each tribe would receive, Simeon's descendants were absorbed into Judah's tribe, receiving nothing for themselves. And Levi's descendants also received no land of their own, but their people lived in 48 towns and the surrounding pasturelands (see Joshua 19:1, 9 and 14:4 or 21:4).

After sharing this story, ask—

• **Using Simeon and Levi as an example, what are some reasons we shouldn't take revenge?** (Revenge tends to escalate and can easily get out of control; revenge hurts its victims, which is why it feels so good at the time; revenge causes sinful behavior; revenge has long-term effects on people besides the revenge-taker and the victim (Simeon and Levi's descendants didn't kill those men, but they lost any chance at owning some great pieces of land).)

• **If this event had occurred in modern times (and in a culture where women aren't viewed as property), what could Simeon and Levi have done differently to help**

Dinah during this difficult time? *(Talk to her about how she felt about Shechem; prayed for her and with her; found a counselor or support group for Dinah to talk to; cooperated fully with the local law enforcement agencies to get Shechem prosecuted and convicted for his crime.)*

Now divide into smaller groups (preferably with an adult leader in each one to facilitate) and hand out copies of Wildpage 2.1—**Our Way or His Way?** (page 22) and pencils or pens to the students. Have the groups read and summarize the passages on the left side of the sheet first. It would save time if they divided up the readings and summarized them for the rest of the group before moving on to the next part.

Next they should read the passages listed on the right side of the worksheet and try to make the best match possible between the biblical story of revenge and how the Bible says we should respond. (Answers: 1) B or E; 2) A; 3) D; 4) C or E.)

After about 7 or 10 minutes, go over the answers with everyone. If a group comes up with different pairings than the answers listed here, ask them to explain why they matched the ones they did.

Ask the students to share any thoughts or insights they have about any of the stories of revenge. To keep things moving, small group leaders should do their best to answer any questions the students have about what took place in each situation.

LET YOUR CONSCIENCE BE YOUR GUIDE

Read Matthew 5:38-42 out loud to the group (it's printed for you at the beginning of this lesson). Ask the students to give you ideas for ways to rewrite the passage as though it were being said around a junior high hallway in the 21st century. (Write it out on an overhead transparency, PowerPoint slide, chalkboard, whiteboard, or wherever it works best for all to see what you're writing.)

For example, to rewrite the tunic and cloak part, you might change it to, "If someone wants to sue you and take your Hurley T-shirt, let him have your leather jacket as well."

After you have a number of suggestions for new ways to write each section, have the students vote on the ones they like best, then put it all together into a brand new passage.

Now ask—

- **What's up with the teeth and eyes stuff in here?** *(Explain how it comes from Exodus 21:24-25 where it was used to make sure that the punishment fit the crime. It's doubtful that anyone actually lost eyes or teeth because of this rule.)*

- **Why does revenge usually entail an escalation response?** *(For example, Simeon and Levi's reaction to Dinah's rape was to lie, kill, and rob.)*

- **How did Joseph live out the commands in these verses when he was a slave in Egypt and later reunited with his brothers?**

- **What is our reaction when someone chooses *not* to seek revenge against us?**

Staying in the smaller groupings, assign each group one of the descriptions of a possible revenge situation found on Wildpage 2.2—**What Should I Do?** (page 23). Each group should read its assigned description before the small groups divide in half again (I know, right now some of you reading this are thinking, "divide in half again? I've only got 6 kids in my group to begin with!" Okay, okay. Adjust!). Now the small group leaders should ask one half of the small group to come up with a strategy of revenge and the other half to use the biblical principles they just read about to come up with a strategy to avoid taking revenge.

Two people from each group—one from the revenge side and one from the non-revenge side—

a place to write where the whole group can read what you've written: chalkboard, whiteboard, PowerPoint or MediaShout stuff, or an overhead projector and the necessary tools to use it

copies of Wildpage 2.2, **What Should I Do?** (page 23) for each small group

Optional: stereotypical angel and devil costume props, like an aluminum foil halo, white T-shirt, and harp for the angel and a black T-shirt, some red horns, a red cape, some dark sunglasses for the devil should be prepared to go up front and try to persuade a leader or student volunteer to do what they suggest to solve the dilemma. Instruct them to picture in their minds the popular cartoon image of an angel and a devil sitting on a person's shoulders.

After you've given the groups enough time to work on their ideas, ask for a student (or adult) volunteer to come forward. If you're using the suggested props and costumes, have the angel and devil get into costume, then position them on either side of the volunteer.

Ask the volunteer to read the description aloud. Once finished, the small group representatives can start trying to sway the volunteer. You can flip a coin to see whether the angel or the devil gets to go first in each case. Give each of them about a minute to work on the volunteer, then ask the conflicted person to share with everyone whether or not he'll choose to take revenge and why he made that choice. You could also have the rest of the youth group take a vote (by show of hands) as to which course of action the person should take.

After every group's representatives have taken a turn, ask—

- **Which responses were easier to come up with for this exercise—revenge or forgiveness?**
- **What actions by another person consistently make you think about striking back at them?** (gossiping, lying about you, using physical violence against you, teasing, stealing, leaving you out of activities)
- **What actions are you more likely to forgive and forget?**
- **What's the difference between the actions you can forgive and the ones you can't?**
- **Why is it so tough for people to forgive and forget?**
- **What would life be like for us if God sought revenge against us every time we did something against him?**

Redisplay the list of grievances and responses you wrote down at the beginning of the lesson for everyone to see. Next to the "Response" column, add a third heading—"The Daring Response." Ask students to think about the aggravating situations that were discussed earlier and come up with some better, more God-pleasing ways to respond in each case.

Using the back of one of their Wildpages (or a new piece of paper that you've provided for them) each person should write two column headings across the top of the paper: "It Really Bugged Me When…" and "God Wants Me To…" Encourage the students to think of at least two aggravating situations—some way they've been hurt by another person but just can't let it go—and write them down in the first column.

After you've given them a few moments to make a list in column one, ask the students to reflect on the various ways God says we should deal with the people who've wronged us. Have them write down some positive ways they could deal with the people in these two (or more) situations. They can have more than one idea for each thing listed in column one.

Now tell them they're going to have to make a gutsy decision. First they must pick one of the situations in column one and put a circle around it. Now they must pick one of the responses written in the second column and circle it to show they're committed to choose that course of action this week.

You may want to go so far as to have the kids choose an accountability partner, someone they trust that they can show their circled responses to and then rely on that person to help them stick with their choice—whatever it may be—in the days and weeks to come.

If some students aren't ready to make this kind of commitment, ask them to keep thinking about it after they leave the group. Encourage them to pray about it and talk to you or their small group leader about it some more.

End with a time of prayer. Thank God for the many positive and negative examples he's given to us in his Word regarding revenge and how we can reflect on them before we decide how to respond when someone hurts us. Ask God to guide the students in the coming week as they live up to the commitments they've made today to choose a godly response in the midst of pain. ✌

You'll Need

✌ blank paper for each student
✌ pencils or pens for each student

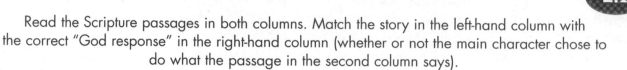

Our Way or His Way?

Read the Scripture passages in both columns. Match the story in the left-hand column with the correct "God response" in the right-hand column (whether or not the main character chose to do what the passage in the second column says).

STORIES OF REVENGE IN THE BIBLE

_____ 1. Brotherly love? (2 Samuel 3:17-30)

_____ 2. Samson outfoxes the Philistines. (Judges 15:1-17)

_____ 3. From Egypt, with love. (Genesis 37:12-36; 45:1-15)

_____ 4. Esther's banquet serves up some just desserts for Haman. (Esther 3:2-11, 4:1-8; 5—7)

GOD'S RESPONSE

A. "Do not say, 'I'll do to him as he has done to me; I'll pay that man back for what he did.'" (Proverbs 24:29)

B. "'Do not seek revenge or bear a grudge against one of your people, but love your neighbor as yourself. I am the Lord.'" (Leviticus 19:18)

C. "Through patience a ruler can be persuaded, and a gentle tongue can break a bone...If your enemy is hungry, give him food to eat; if he is thirsty, give him water to drink. In doing this, you will heap burning coals on his head, and the Lord will reward you." (Proverbs 25:15, 21-22)

D. "To this you were called because Christ suffered for you, leaving you an example, that you should follow in his steps. 'He committed no sin, and no deceit was found in his mouth.' When they hurled their insults at him, he did not retaliate; when he suffered, he made no threats. Instead he entrusted himself to him who judges justly." (1 Peter 2:21-23)

E. "Do not take revenge, my friends, but leave room for God's wrath, for it is written: 'It is mine to avenge; I will repay,' says the Lord."(Romans 12:19)

What Should I Do?

2.2

Revenge Situation #1:

Hi! My name is Luis, and I have a problem. I'm the star pitcher for my school's baseball team. We're in the middle of the biggest conference game of the season, and the other team's pitcher just hit one of our batters with a pitch. The guys and I were discussing it in the dugout, and they're sure it was deliberate because this other team usually plays dirty. So now my teammates are telling me I should hit one of *their* batters during the next inning because that's how they do it in the major leagues. I don't feel right about it. I mean I'm not the one who got hit by the pitch. And I could get thrown out of the game or start a fight between the teams. What should I do?

Revenge Situation #2:

Hello. I'm Ruby. I got my driver's license three months ago, and my mom finally agreed to let me take some of my friends out driving tonight. We've been cruising around town for an hour or so and decided to go over to the next town to see a movie. So I just pulled onto the freeway, and this guy in a pickup truck wouldn't let me in his lane! He kept speeding up whenever I tried to move over, and then he finally sped on ahead of me. I almost drove off the road because of him! My friends are really shaken up, but they keep telling me I should follow him and cut in front of *him*. I'm still new to this whole driving thing, and their plan sounds kind of dangerous. What should I do?

Revenge Situation #3:

Hey! My name is Dakota but my friends call me "Dak." Speaking of my friends, they're right over there cooking up a big scheme to get back at our history teacher, Ms. Lopez. She caught some of my buddies cheating during an exam last week, but she didn't know how many of us were in on it. So she sent all of us to the principal's office, and we were suspended for three days. Today is our first day back at school. Our parents are so mad at us! We've all been grounded for three weeks—no TV, no video games, no phone calls, and no hanging out with the guys after school for almost a month! I wasn't cheating so some of the guys think I should get Ms. Lopez back for punishing me for no reason. They're talking about sneaking out tonight and egging her house, throwing toilet paper into her trees, and soaping her car. They're even talking about kidnapping her dog for a ransom! What should I do?

Revenge Situation #4:

What's up? I'm Kaneesha. My boyfriend Jamad and I broke up two weeks ago. He wasn't treating me right and my friend, Danika, convinced me that I'd be better off without him. So I broke up with him. Well, I found out from another girlfriend, Shanise, that she saw Jamad and Danika making out by the locker rooms after the football game last night! How could they do this to me? I told Shanise that I was going to call Danika and Jamad and let them know that I know what's going on, and I'm not going to take this. She said there are better ways to get even with them, like telling their parents that I know those two are having sex (even though I don't know that for sure, I've only heard a few rumors). What should I do?

Revenge Situation #5:

My name is Kim Jung Hien. My father owns a small Korean grocery store where I work after school. My older brother, Kim Jung Yul, also works for my father. He helps deliver groceries to our sick or elderly customers. Last week Yul had to go to a rough part of town to make a delivery. Before he got back to the truck, someone broke into it, stole all of the groceries out of the back, and sprayed graffiti all over it. It was his first delivery of the night, so my father lost a lot of money because of the stolen food and having to get the truck repainted. I heard Yul's friends talking about how they're sure this one neighborhood gang is responsible for what happened. They're planning to go find those guys and damage one of their cars with baseball bats and knives. Yul says I should go with them to defend our father's honor and let these guys know they can't mess with us. What should I do?

Go Long

"Do not store up for yourselves treasures on earth, where moth and rust destroy, and where thieves break in and steal. But store up for yourselves treasures in heaven, where moth and rust do not destroy, and where thieves do not break in and steal. For where your treasure is, there your heart will be also."

Matthew 6:19-21

GOALS

Students Will—

- Understand (we hope!) the abstract concept of investing in eternal things
- Consider varying ways young teens can make eternal investments
- Brainstorm three ways they can make eternal investments, and choose one to take as a dare

PLAY THE MARKET

Have your students form teams of 2-3 (larger if your group is large). Before the meeting, gather the financial section of a newspaper for three or four different days. Photocopy a portion of the stock market reports and have one copy of each for each team. It doesn't matter which part you copy, as long as it's the same for each day.

Ask your group if anyone can quickly explain how the stock market works. If no one is able to provide an even remotely satisfactory answer, say something like: Companies that want money to use to grow their businesses can sell off little portions of their companies to investors. That's what stock ownership is: buying a little piece of the company. If the company does well, your little piece of ownership is worth more. If the company does poorly, your little piece of ownership is, of course, worth less.

You'll Need

- photocopies of one page from the financial section of a newspaper (the stock listings) from more than one day, and a writing utensil for each team
- Optional: a small candy prize for the winning team

Hand out the copy of the earliest stock listings you have (It is important that you have them in chronological order!). Have the teams look over the sheet and choose one stock they want to "buy." Most of your kids will have no idea what all the numbers mean—that doesn't matter at all. Most of us wouldn't recognize the code names for companies even if we knew the names of the companies! Of course, you might have some stock-wizard kid in your group who already has investments and could run circles around you in this area (young teens never cease to surprise and amaze me)! Each team needs to agree on *one* stock to "buy." Have the teams circle it on the sheets.

After they finish, pass out the second set of copies (from at least one day later). Instruct the groups to find their stock and note the change in value. The changes in value are reported as positive or negative changes or occasionally show no change. For instance, one group's stock may show a change of "plus 10," while another group's stock may have dropped 1 1/8. Those are percentages of change. Again, they should circle their stock.

Find out which group had the most positive change and which group had the most negative change.

Then pass out the third round of copies (from yet a later date). You get the idea. You can play as many rounds as you want (three would probably be the minimum). At the end have the groups total up the amount of change in their stocks from beginning to end, and find out which groups had the most change positively and negatively.

Consider awarding a small candy prize to the team who had the most positive change, and a funny prize (like one small bag of M&Ms) to the team with the worst overall change.

ETERNAL INVESTMENT COUNSELORS, INC.

Before your meeting begins, select three students (or adult volunteers) to participate in a reader's theater drama. Sure, it's really a regular drama. But the participants don't need to prepare ahead of time, other than to read through their lines once or twice. The script (**Eternal Investment Counselors, Inc.**) is on page 28 at the end of this lesson.

You'll Need

- three volunteer readers (make sure they're kids or adults who can read fairly well), and four copies of the **Eternal Investment Counselors, Inc.**, reader's theater.
- Bibles (or some way to show the passage).

There are four parts:
Narrator (you, or another adult leader)
Gabe, the investment counselor
Jim and Jill, a brother and sister looking to make an investment

Place three chairs in front of your room as a set: one facing the other two, as if there were a desk in the middle. If you have a table to place in the middle as a desk, that would simply add to the realism of this drama (note sarcasm).

Here's what I tried to do when scripting this lame little play: As you know, young teens are still not great (read: lousy) at abstract thinking. Just last night, my wife's small group of girls, when asked if they are "more like New York or more like Colorado" simply couldn't make the mental jump. They could only think in terms of which state they'd rather visit. So, talking about "making eternal investments" is, to say the least, *way* abstract. I barely understand it! The drama is an opportunity to name the concrete thoughts many of your students will be surfacing ("I don't understand," "I thought we were talking about investing money," "What does investing in people or prayer look like?" "How does it work?"). And it moves to explanations thast will hopefully help them round the corner to a loose grasp on this abstract spiritual concept. Jesus sure loved metaphors and similes!

Introduce the three actors, and let the Tony-Award-winning performance begin!

Afterward, have students turn to the passage referred to at the end of the drama: Matthew 6:19-21.

Do not store up for yourselves treasures on earth, where moth and rust destroy, and where thieves break in and steal. But store up for yourselves treasures in heaven, where moth and rust do not destroy, and where thieves do not break in and steal. For where your treasure is, there your heart will be also.

Then ask these questions:

• **Let's start with the basics: what does it mean to invest in something?** *You analyze and decide where to place your resources (money, but also could be time, effort, or reputation!) in the expectation of assisting growth.*

• **So, when someone invests in the stock market, what are they hoping will happen?** *The company they invest in will grow, and they'll get more money in return.*

• **What other kinds of things can you invest in?** *Really, almost anything.*

• **Besides money, what can you *use* to invest?** *Time, prayer, service, love, attention, listening, understanding, cheese puffs.*

• **So what does it mean to invest in eternal things? What's Jesus daring us to do here?** *Put our time and energy into things God cares about.*

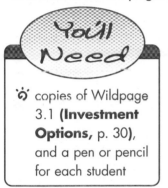

INVESTMENT OPTIONS

You'll Need
- copies of Wildpage 3.1 (**Investment Options,** p. 30), and a pen or pencil for each student

Hand out copies of **Investment Options** (Wildpage 3.1), and a pen or pencil to each student. Walk them through the instructions on the page. First they should read the list and check all the boxes that are, by any reasonable definition, an investment. In other words, they should be checking financial investments, selfish investment (like "spend a lot of time thinking about popularity"), and eternal investments.

Then, after they've had a chance to complete this, have them look back over the list again, as it says, and customize the list into four categories.

After your group completes this, quickly read through the list and ask the group which category they placed it in. If you're pinched for time, choose a couple examples from each category. Continue to watch closely for understanding: are your kids grasping the abstract concept of this dare?

the God-stuff category), or new ones they think up. Important: many of your kids could think of an eternal investment they're already making. Challenge them to think of something *new*, not just something they're already doing. It's not much of a "dare acceptance" if they just continue doing exactly what they already do!

You'll Need
- Wildpage 3.1 that you just used in the last exercise, and writing utensils.

After they've had a few minutes to write three ideas, have them choose one they will accept as a dare from Jesus. They should circle that investment idea and put stars by it—maybe even sign next to it as a commitment. Ask a few students to share their ideas.

Close your time with a group prayer where kids finish sentences you begin. In other words, you say: **God, help us to spend less time on worthless investments like...** (and they should add phrases to complete this prayer sentence). Then you could pray: **God, help us to invest in the things that please you, like...** (and they can read the dares they've circled).

MY INVESTMENT

Transition to the personal dare by having students complete the question at the bottom of **Investment Options** (Wildpage 3.1, p. 30). Encourage your students to think of eternal investments they can really do—ones they would actually consider making. These can be ideas from the big honkin' list they've just completed (hopefully, from

Eternal Investment Counselors, Inc.

Characters:

- **Narrator**
- **Jim**
- **Gabe**
- **Jill**

Narrator: The scene begins as Jim and Jill, two 20-something siblings enter the front door of the Eternal Investment Company.

Gabe (standing): Hello. Welcome to the Eternal Investment Company. How can I help you today?

Jim (shaking Gabe's hand): My sister and I have just come into an inheritance, and we would like to invest in something.

Jill: But we don't know much about investing, and we really need someone we can trust to advise us.

Gabe (all characters sit down): That's why I'm here. I'd love to help you. And I base my advice on the highest authority in the investment world.

Jim: Who would that be?

Gabe: We'll get to that eventually. But first, tell me what your goals are.

Jill: Well, it seems to us that the smartest thing would be to invest in something that will be safe—not something too high-risk.

Jim: Yeah, we thought about just hiding our investment in a shoe box in the closet. But that's not very safe, since someone could break into our home and steal it!

Gabe: Good thinking!

Jill: And we thought about just putting it in a bank, but it doesn't seem we'd get much return that way.

Gabe: That's true! So…what did you say your goal is?

Jim: I guess our goal is to get a high return on our investment.

Gabe: OK. Have you thought about investing in people?

Jill: You mean, like, investing in a company with lots of employees?

Gabe: No, I mean actually investing in people. In individuals. Build into people with your life. Love them with God's love. There's always a great return on that investment.

Jim: I don't get it. Why would that do any good?

Gabe: Or maybe you should consider investing in prayer?

Jill: What?

Gabe: Yeah, prayer is a fantastic investment!

Jim: Is there a company that handles that?

Gabe: Well, it's not exactly a company. But the group that handles your prayers can, again, guarantee a great return.

Jim: I'm still confused.

Gabe: Another great investment for long-range return is serving.

Jill: You mean a company in the service industry? Like hotels or food service?

Gabe: No, I mean you two actually serving others.

Jill: What would the return be on that?

Gabe: Long-range returns! God takes your investment and turns it into amazing results in peoples' lives!

Jim: Wait—are you an investment counselor or some kind of religious fanatic?

Gabe: I'm an investment counselor! And I want to see you invest in the best ways possible.

Jim: What was that authority you were talking about earlier?

Gabe: Well, the Bible. The authority is actually God!

Jill: OK, this is getting really weird.

Gabe: You see, the Bible makes it clear that the best investment plan ever is to invest in heaven.

Jill: Heaven sells stock?

Gabe: Well, sort of. If you choose to invest in the things that God values—loving people, reaching out to them with God's truth, prayer, serving others, spending time with God—you can't lose.

Jim: But how will that make us any money?

Gabe: Oh, I didn't say anything about making money! Money burns, gets lost, and won't last. And all the things you can buy with money—stuff—that will all go away too. But eternal things...now those are good investments.

Jill: So what are you saying we should do with our money—just put it in a shoe box in the closet?

Gabe: Of course not! You can invest your money in God's kingdom also. But I'm talking about investing much more than money. The money you have is just a small part of what you can and should be investing.

Jim: OK, so let's pretend for a minute that we take your investment advice. What will the results be?

Gabe: Your life will have more meaning and purpose. You'll grow in your relationship with God. And God will use your investments of time, service, prayer, *and* money to help other people.

Jill: Why is that eternal?

Gabe: Because when a person's life is changed, the change is forever. The work that God does—that you invest in—doesn't go up and down like the stock market. God promises that the results will last forever!

Jim: I think I hear what you're saying. But it's really not what we were expecting to hear. We're going to have to think about this and get back to you.

Gabe (standing, and shaking their hands): OK, well, I'd love to hear from you again. Do you guys have a Bible?

Jim and Jill: Yeah.

Gabe: I challenge you to go home and read Matthew 6:19-21. It's a dare from Jesus about your investments.

Narrator: Jim and Jill leave a bit confused with lots of things to think about.

Investment Options

Put a check mark in the box next to ways you could invest (you might not choose to invest in them, but mark the ones that are reasonable investment ideas, good or bad or neutral). **3.1**

❑ Put money in a bank account.

❑ Play the stock market.

❑ Serve in the nursery of your church as an investment into the lives of little kids and their parents.

❑ Get an atlas of the world, and spend time praying for the people of a different country every day.

❑ Begin an e-mail relationship with the teenage son or daughter of a missionary.

❑ Stockpile gold!

❑ Chocolate-covered raisins: the investment of the future.

❑ Use lots of effort on popularity: now there's an investment that will last as long as… well… not very long.

❑ Volunteer, maybe with some friends, to serve meals at a homeless shelter.

❑ Buy land where you expect a city to expand.

❑ Spend time in silence, listening to God.

❑ Get into the Bible—God's Word—and start reading it regularly.

❑ Volunteer to tutor at an after-school program, or a friend struggling in a subject you understand.

❑ Never, ever throw anything away. You just never know what will become valuable someday.

❑ Use your gifts and abilities to help your church (help with the church Web site, sing in the choir).

❑ Worry and stress: two very popular investments these days!

❑ Commit to praying regularly for three friends who don't know Jesus.

❑ See if you can create the world's largest rubber-band ball, then charge people to see it.

Now, go back and customize the list in these four ways:
• Cross out the ideas that are just plain stupid or weird.
• Put a dollar sign on the ideas that are about investing money for personal gain.
• Put a dotted line under the ideas that are selfish—ways some young teens invest time and energy in things that are poor investments.
• And circle the ideas that are eternal investments: investments in God-stuff.

Now come up with three more ideas of ways that you could invest in God-stuff (they can be new ideas, or ones from the list above):

1.

2.

3.

30

Don't Waste Your Time

"Therefore I tell you, do not worry about your life, what you will eat or drink; or about your body, what you will wear. Is not life more important than food, and the body more important than clothes? Look at the birds of the air; they do not sow or reap or store away in barns, and yet your heavenly Father feeds them. Are you not much more valuable than they? Who of you by worrying can add a single hour to his life?

"And why do you worry about clothes? See how the lilies of the field grow. They do not labor or spin. Yet I tell you that not even Solomon in all his splendor was dressed like one of these. If that is how God clothes the grass of the field, which is here today and tomorrow is thrown into the fire, will he not much more clothe you, O you of little faith? So do not worry, saying, `What shall we eat?' or `What shall we drink?' or `What shall we wear?' For the pagans run after all these things, and your heavenly Father knows that you need them. But seek first his kingdom and his righteousness, and all these things will be given to you as well. Therefore do not worry about tomorrow, for tomorrow will worry about itself. Each day has enough trouble of its own."

Matthew 6:25-34

GOALS

Students Will—

- Understand that worrying about things can have a negative effect on them and the people they care about
- Realize that God wants them to trust him and trade in their worries and anxiety for his perfect peace
- Figure out ways to view their worries with the proper perspective

YOU DON'T KNOW THE HALF OF IT!

Before your group gathers, take a look at Wildpage 4.1— **We'll Cross that Bridge When Pigs Fly?** (pp. 35-36). It contains 36 old sayings from around the globe to get you started. You can either make copies of this sheet (you need to have enough pairs of sayings cards to tape one card to the back of each kid at the beginning of the game), or come up with your own silly sayings and write them on index cards. If your group is large, it's not a problem to have more than one copy of a saying (so that two or three or more kids have it). If your group is small, don't use them all!

To play this little mixer game, students will start by pairing off and asking each other what their card says. After they've read the cards aloud to each other, the two should talk about whether or not their two halves make a complete saying. If they believe they do, then they should run and sit down somewhere along the wall of the room until the rest of the players finish. If not, then the players should move on, find a new partner, and exchange card information again.

Put a little pressure on your kids during this activity. Give them an insanely short amount of time in which to find their partner. Promise them an extravagant prize to the quickest (and, of course, correct) team. Put fake beginnings and endings on

You'll Need

- copies of Wildpage 4.1— **We'll Cross that Bridge When Pigs Fly?** (pp. 35-36)
- Scotch tape

some kids' backs so they never find a partner. Play really loud, driving music during the game or repeatedly play "Don't Worry, Be Happy," that annoying tune sung by Bobby McFerrin in the '80s, until the kids want to scream. Try anything you can think of to get their adrenaline pumping and create a little bit of panic (which is closely related to our topic of worry).

Make sure you notice which kids make a match first. After everyone is finished, have the pairs read aloud their cards, then tell them if they're right or wrong. Consider tossing a small candy prize to those pairs who matched early *and* had a correct match.

Another option is to have the student pairs check in with a leader when they think they have the correct match. If they're wrong, the leader sends them back into the fray to find a new partner and start the process all over again.

When the game ends, share the right answers with the group, as well as the culture or country that it comes from. Then ask—

- **Which saying seemed the weirdest to you?**
- **Which saying made you laugh?**
- **Which one made the most sense to you?**
- **Have you ever heard one of these sayings before?**
- **Do your parents, grandparents, or anyone else in your family have a saying or two that they use regularly? (Get some examples.)**
- **How did that saying get started in your family?**

- 😀 a place to write a list that everyone can see
- 😀 something to write with

"We will cross that bridge when we come to it."

"Worrying never changed anything."

"Worry often gives a small thing a big shadow." (Swedish proverb)

"The reason why worry kills more people than work is that more people worry than work." (Robert Frost)

"Don't worry about the world coming to an end today. It's already tomorrow in Australia." (Charles Schulz)

"Sorrow looks back, worry looks around, faith looks up."

Then ask—

- **How do your friends or parents respond to your worries?**
- **How do their responses or reactions make you feel?**
- **How could they respond in a more helpful way?**
- **What can *you* do to stop letting worry take control of your life?**

Ask student volunteers to read the following passages aloud (just use a few of them if your time is short):

- **Proverbs 3:5-6**
- **Proverbs 12:25**
- **Proverbs 14:26**
- **Proverbs 24:19-20**
- **2 Corinthians 7:5-7**
- **Philippians 4:6-7**
- **1 Peter 5:6-7**

WHY SHOULD I WORRY?

Ask your students if they know any sayings about worry. After you get a few ideas from them, read the following examples aloud. After you read each one, ask if anyone can tell you the meaning. (Note: It would help to have these sayings written down where the kids can see them as you read them aloud.)

After each Scripture is read, ask the following questions and write down a list (where everyone can see) of better ways to deal with our worries, according to these passages.

- **What does the Bible say we should do instead of worry?**
- **How could doing this help you to stop worrying?**
- **Have any of you tried doing this? (If anyone has, ask them to share what happened with the group.)**

WORRY CAN BECOME CHILD'S PLAY

Before your youth group meeting, preview and choose one of the suggested children's stories about worry in the You'll Need list. Yeah, I know, this suggestion takes a little more prep work for you (and will be really difficult if you're preparing your lesson 10 minutes before your group meets!).

Before you read a children's book out loud to your group, make a point of letting your students know that you aren't trying to treat them like little kids. On the contrary, some of the best truth is found in children's books. So they should just sit back and enjoy the story.

When you've finished reading, ask the students—

- **Who can relate to the main character(s) and their worries in this story?** *(Ask for a show of hands. Then ask for a few volunteers to share how and why they can relate.)*

Now ask—

- **How many of you worry about stuff?** *(Ask for another show of hands—if they're honest, they'll all raise their hands!)*

- **What kinds of things do junior highers worry about?**

- **When you get worried, how do you feel physically?** *(Sick to your stomach, sweaty palms, can't sleep, headache)*

- **How do you feel mentally?** *(Can't concentrate on anything, daydream a lot, don't notice things like you usually do)*

- **How about emotionally?** *(Moody, irritable, cry at the drop of a hat, want to be alone, feel depressed)*

You'll Need

- ☺ one of the following children's books (for ages four to eight): *Mrs. Meyer the Bird* by Wolf Erlbruch, *Wemberly Worried* by Kevin Henkes, *The Worrywarts* by Pamela Duncan Edwards, or *The Worry Stone* by Marianna Dengler (All four are available at Amazon.com and could probably be found at your local library or book store as well.)
- ☺ paper and pencils or pens for each small group

- **And spiritually?** *(Feel like God is far away, see no reason to pray, the last thing you feel like doing is opening your Bible or going to church and seeing all of the carefree Christians around you)*

- **How do you treat your friends and family when you're worried?** *(Snap at them, ignore them, smother them, whine at them)*

- **When you're worrying about stuff, how do the thoughts, attitudes, and actions (treatment of others and yourself) just described help the situation you're worried about?**

- **On the other hand, how do your thoughts, attitudes, and actions make the situation worse than before you started to worry?**

Optional Idea
Confessions of a Worrywart

If you can't find one of the children's books mentioned, here's an optional idea where the students come up with their own story about how they act when they're worried.

On a blank sheet of paper, have students write numbers from one through 18 in a column. Look at Wildpage 4.2 (page 37), and tell the students what to write next to each number—each student's name or nickname in #1; their school mascot in #2, and so on. Give them a little bit of time to think of each item.

After everyone finishes, hand out copies of **Confessions of a Worrywart** (page 37) and ask the students to copy the words from their list into the appropriate spaces on the worksheet. There should be a healthy dose of distraction and chatter during this exercise (as if there isn't all the time in your group!). Choose a few student volunteers and ask them to read their mad lib aloud.

Now say something like: **The part of your mad lib that is supposed to describe the way you worry probably doesn't resemble the way you handle worry in real life. These stories are meant to**

You'll Need

- ☺ paper for each student
- ☺ pencils or pens for each student
- ☺ copies of Wildpage 4.2—**Confessions of a Worrywart** (p. 37)

be stupid. But worrying too much over things you can't control can have a serious effect on your life. (To finish this exercise use the discussion questions at the end of the "Truth in Action" section, beginning with "How many of you worry about stuff?".)

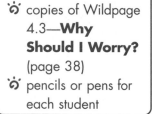

WHY SHOULD I WORRY?

Ask students to list some examples of better ways to deal with worry that you've already talked about. Some ideas are:

- **Focus on thinking about the present in small amounts of time—the next hour, the next afternoon—instead of looking so far ahead that you end up with a head full of things to worry about.**
- **Do something instead of just dwelling on things that could go wrong.**
  - **Talk to someone about your worries and get a fresh perspective.**
  - **Make a list of worst-case scenarios about the situation so you can see that the possible outcomes aren't so bad, laugh at how ridiculous they are, or pray about them and let God take it from there.**

Point out to your students that they can also use these worry-free ideas to help their friends and family members when they're worried.

Hand out copies of Wildpage 4.3—**Why Should I Worry?** (page 38) to each student. Ask them to silently work on their sheets for a few minutes. When they finish, ask for a show of hands as to how many took the dare and signed their sheet to show they're committed to stop worrying about something this week.

You'll Need

- ☞ copies of Wildpage 4.3—**Why Should I Worry?** (page 38)
- ☞ pencils or pens for each student

End your time with prayer, specifically praying for some of the worries your students have shared with the group during this lesson. Ask God to remind them of his presence in their lives when they feel worried and show them better ways to respond to their concerns.

In the story *The Worry Stone* one of the characters describes how rubbing a stone helped ease some of the worries in her heart. If you used this story earlier in the lesson, then remind the students about what was said about the stone and hand out smooth "worry stones" to each student to take home with them. Even if you didn't choose to use *The Worry Stone* story during this lesson, you can tell your students that the stones in their hands can serve as a reminder that the Lord is their rock—"He who fears the Lord has a secure fortress…" (Proverbs 14:26). As God's children we can take our worries to the Lord any time and all the time, and he will give us his guidance and perfect peace.

Give your students one more saying to think about as they go. This one comes from Confucius, "The gem cannot be polished without friction, nor man perfected without trials." This basically tells us that the tough times are for our own good, which is what the Bible also tells us. This saying should encourage us to look for the bright side of our worrisome situations—tough times are going to mold and shape us so we look more like Christ! That's something to get pumped about!

Answers to game on page 35 (☞)

From Switzerland: In calm water…every ship has a good captain.

From England: It is no use fishing…in front of the net.

From China: Almonds come to those who…have no teeth.

From Bulgaria: Other people's eggs have …two yolks.

From Switzerland: Strange bread…makes the cheeks red.

From Jamaica: It's hard to get butter out of…a dog's throat.

From France: A stick is a good…peacemaker.

From Kenya: Beans come from the place…where the beans are.

From the Ukraine: Every road has…two directions.

From Zimbabwe: The cow licks the one…that licks it.

From Surinam: When the ground is hot…the worm stays in the dirt.

From Finland: The water is the same…on both sides of the boat.

From India: A coconut shell full of water…is an ocean to an ant.

From Samoa: I am sitting in a…cranky boat.

From Mongolia: The dog only starts to swim when…the water reaches its chin.

From Malaysia: Poling down stream makes…the crocodiles laugh.

From Wales: A stone will…swim to the bottom.

From Bantu: Water is never…tired of flowing.

W I L D P A G E

We'll Cross that Bridge When Pigs Fly?

Make enough copies of these pages so you'll have one card to tape to each student's back.
Cut apart the cards, and tape them to the students as they enter your youth group room.
The answers to this game can be found at the bottom of page 34.

4.1a

THE FIRST HALF OF THE SAYINGS

From Switzerland: **In calm water...**	From Zimbabwe: **The cow licks the one...**
From England: **It is no use fishing...**	From Surinam: **When the ground is hot...**
From China: **Almonds come to those who...**	From Finland: **The water is the same...**
From Bulgaria: **Other people's eggs have ...**	From India: **A coconut shell full of water...**
From Switzerland: **Strange bread...**	From Samoa: **I am sitting in a...**
From Jamaica: **It's hard to get butter out of...**	From Mongolia: **The dog only starts to swim when...**
From France: **A stick is a good...**	From Malaysia: **Poling down stream makes...**
From Kenya: **Beans come from the place...**	From Wales: **A stone will...**
From the Ukraine: **Every road has...**	From Bantu: **Water is never...**

35

THE SECOND HALF OF THE SAYINGS

...every ship has a good captain.

...that licks it.

...in front of the net.

...the worm stays in the dirt.

...have no teeth.

...on both sides of the boat.

...two yolks.

...is an ocean to an ant.

...makes the cheeks red.

...cranky boat.

...a dog's throat.

...the water reaches its chin.

...peacemaker.

...the crocodiles laugh.

...where the beans are.

...swim to the bottom.

...two directions.

...tired of flowing

Confessions of a Worrywart

Transfer your word list to the blanks below (in the same order).

My name is _____**#1**_____ (student's first name) and I'm a _____**#2**_____ (your school's mascot). Go

_____**#3**_____ s!!! (school mascot again) Anyway, things are pretty tough at _____**#4**_____ (name of

your school). Every _____**#5**_____ (general time of day: morning, noon, afternoon, evening) our teacher,

_____**#6**_____ (name of least favorite teacher), makes us do _____**#7**_____ (large number)

_____**#8**_____ s (a P.E. exercise) before class begins. And during our lunch period they serve

____**#9**____ and _____**#10**_____ (two least favorite foods) every other day!

Now, just when I thought things couldn't get any worse, _____**#11**_____ (favorite teacher), who is

SO cool, gave us a final project that's worth half our grade! I'm trying not to worry about it, but it's a really

big deal. It's the first thing I think about in the morning when I'm eating my bowl of _____**#12**_____ (breakfast

cereal). And when I see my friend _____**#13**_____ (first name of a friend) at school, we always ask each

other, "Have you started working on the project yet?"

When I'm worried about something my head _____**#14**_____ (present tense action verb), my heart

____**#15**____ (present tense action verb, different from the last one), and my hands _____**#16**_____ (another

present tense action verb). But the weirdest thing of all is that my nose sounds like a _____**#17**_____

(something that makes a strange noise), and my eyes cross until everything looks _____**#18**_____ (color) to

me! How can I fix this problem? If my body keeps doing these crazy things, I'll never get my project done in

time!

37

1. List your top five worries below.

2. What have you done to deal with these five concerns of yours? How have you managed to change the situation?

3. Which of the five situations you listed in number one are too big for God to handle?

4. If you could stop worrying about one of these five things, which one would you choose (circle it)?

5. What can you start doing today to stop worrying about that issue (list at least three things)?

6. Put a star next to the one thing you plan to do in the next week to help lessen your anxiety about the concern you circled in number four. Now sign the bottom of this page to show you're committed to stop worrying about at least this one thing starting this week.

Don't Be Foolish!

"Therefore everyone who hears these words of mine and puts them into practice is like a wise man who built his house on the rock. The rain came down, the streams rose, and the winds blew and beat against that house; yet it did not fall, because it had its foundation on the rock. But everyone who hears these words of mine and does not put them into practice is like a foolish man who built his house on sand. The rain came down, the streams rose, and the winds blew and beat against that house, and it fell with a great crash."

Matthew 7:24-27

GOALS

Students Will—

- **Look at how Jesus uses a story to issue a dare**
- **Understand why it's wise to apply Jesus' teachings to our lives**
- **Choose a wise application to a Jesus teaching to carry out this week**

DARE STORIES

You'll Need

ö nothing but the strange calling you've received to love young teens! Oh, I guess that's not completely true—you'll need a blank piece of paper and pen for each group of four students.

This lesson starts off on a different tack. Normally, the first step of the lesson is used to hook students into the subject. But I love the method Jesus uses to issue this dare: a story. You have to read between the lines a bit to realize it's a dare! But the whole idea of using a story to dare someone to do something is fairly abstract. All that to say: we're using the opening exercise to introduce the abstract idea of using a story to issue a dare, *not* to introduce the subject of obeying Jesus (that will come later).

Have students form groups of about four. If your group has six kids—modify. If your group has 350 kids—modify. Give a blank piece of paper and a pen to each group (just one per group).

Before you give any instructions, read this story: **If you want to be cool, you'll do what John did. He always wanted to skydive. So as soon as he was old enough, he went on his first tandem jump, where you're strapped to the jump instructor. Eventually he became a jump instructor himself. And then he invented a whole new way to jump without using a parachute—just using the currents of the warm air rising from the ground. That's what John did.**

Now ask:

- **I want you to think for a minute about what I just did. Don't think about the story too much. Think about what someone might be trying to accomplish by telling a story like that. What do you think it might be?** *This is a way-difficult question, and I doubt your kids will get it. Oh, they'll have responses, but probably not the correct one, which is that it's a dare to jump out of planes. But who knows, you might have a future Albert Einstein in your group who nails it. Don't spend much time clarifying answers at this point.*

- **Who can tell me the rules of Truth or Dare?** *You take turns asking another person in the game if they choose "truth" (a question to which they are required to tell the self-revealing truth), or if they choose "dare" (a physical dare they must complete).*

- **Normally, when you dare someone to do something, you just say it. But what would it look like if you used a story to issue a dare?** *This is an open-ended question—there are no right answers.*

- **What if someone came up to you at school and said, "Hey, only the complete losers aren't trying a bit of this awesome pot I'm selling. Like Philip—he said, 'I just say no to drugs!' And Carly, that freak, she was like, 'Oh, I just don't know...' But all the cool kids are trying it.**

- **What's the dare in this story?** *I dare you to buy some pot and try it.*

- **Did the person in the story ever actually offer to sell pot?** *No, it's implied.*

Now give your students instructions to think up, in their groups, a story—just a few sentences long—that could be used to dare someone to do something. It doesn't have to be something negative, like trying drugs. It can be a dare to do anything—but they can't actually come out and say, "I dare you to do this" or "you should try this."

Also instruct them to stay away from making an offer or invitation. You might even take a minute to discuss the difference between an invitation and a dare. Make sure one of the group members acts as a scribe and writes down their work. By the way, it would be SO good to have adult leaders helping these groups!

Give the groups about five minutes to complete their work. Mingle around the groups to make sure they understand the task. Read their work, and make sure it's not an invitation but a dare (this is a bit tricky). After it seems most groups are done, have groups read their stories; then ask the rest of the group to discern the dare in the story.

JESUS THROWS DOWN A STORY

Recruit a handful of kids to play the roles in a short **Spontaneous Melodrama**. They don't have to have any acting ability—just a willingness to ham it up. Be careful in selecting the players for the roles of "wise dude" and "dumb dude." Whoever plays the "dumb dude" *must* be a student with strong self-esteem. In fact, it would be great to have a male adult volunteer play this role. The last thing you want is for some kid to go home thinking he was typecast as the idiot!

Introduce the drama (that word sure is an overstatement!) by explaining that Jesus sometimes gave dares in the form of stories— and this is one of them.

You'll Need

- one copy of the "Jesus Throws Down a Story" **Spontaneous Melodrama** at the end of this lesson for you to read
- Bibles for everyone, or a way to show the primary passage

Now read the script and have the actors play their parts. Pause at natural points for the cast to do their thing. If a character has a line, read it, then have them repeat it in character. If the characters aren't getting into their parts, give them verbal prodding (or cattle prodding, if you prefer).

After the scene is complete, make sure everyone applauds wildly for the cast. Then have everyone turn in their Bibles to Matthew 7:24-27, printed here because we like you:

> *Therefore everyone who hears these words of mine and puts them into practice is like a wise man who built his house on the rock. The rain came down, the streams rose, and the winds blew and beat against that house; yet it did not fall, because it had its foundation on the rock. But everyone who hears these words of mine and does not put them into practice is like a foolish man who built his house on sand. The rain came down, the streams rose, and the winds blew and beat against that house, and it fell with a great crash.*

I believe it's important to let junior highers actually *see* scripture. So don't just read this to them. If you don't have Bibles for everyone (or at least one for every other student), put the passage on a posterboard or PowerPoint slide (or use MediaShout—the coolest presentation software on Planet Earth).

Then ask:

- **What dare do you think Jesus was issuing with this story?** *Quite simply, to obey him. But allow kids to answer in their own words—not just using "church answers."*

- **What does it mean to hear the words of Jesus and put them into practice?** *Applying them to everyday life; allowing his instructions to us to impact the way we live.*

- **According to the story, what happens when you apply Jesus' teachings to your life?** *Like the wise dude, your life will have a strong foundation. In other words, you'll be able to hold on when things get tough—just like the Rock House.*

- **According to the story, what happens when you *don't* apply Jesus' teaching to your life?** *Like the dumb dude, your life won't have a strong foundation. In other words, you won't be able to stand firm when the going gets tough.*

- **What kinds of things do the Wind, Stream and Rain represent in Jesus' dare story?** *Tough times, doubts, challenges to our faith, and temptations.*

a brainstorming session that brings out a wide variety of Jesus' teachings. Be careful that this doesn't just become a list of do's and don'ts (the Pharisees could do that, and they sure weren't considered wise by Jesus standards!). Steer the brainstorming toward things like:

- **Putting love into action**
- **Living with the knowledge that God loves you**
- **Taking a stand for truth and defending people others ignore or mistreat**

Now have your students stand up and move in between two signs you put on your walls before the meeting: one should say "wise teen," and the other—on the opposite wall—should say "dumb teen." Tell the kids you're going to read a handful of examples. Their job is to move to one sign or the other to choose if the teen in the story is wise (applying Jesus' words to her life) or dumb (not applying Jesus' words).

WISE TEENS AND DUMB TEENS

Say something like: **I want to be clear about something here: when we talk about being wise and dumb, we're *not* talking about how smart or intelligent you are. Wisdom is about making good choices. Some really smart people aren't wise because they make dumb choices. And some people who aren't very smart are still very wise, because they make good choices.**

Ask for examples of "Jesus teachings." In other words, what should we *do* if we want to build our lives on a strong foundation like the Wise Dude? Try to lead

Shantell was reading her Bible this morning and came across Jesus' story of the prodigal son—the one who was loved by his father even though he'd totally messed up. So Shantell chose to make a list of the things God forgives her for, then threw it away to represent the fact that those things were gone and in the past. *(Wise teen)*

Gary's mom said something to him yesterday about "loving your neighbor as yourself." Gary knew he didn't love himself very much—so he decided the best thing to do was to forget about other people until he figured out how to take care of himself. *(Dumb teen—he missed the point of the teaching!)*

All her life, Cassidy has heard church people tell her about how Jesus wants us to use the gifts He's given us. Cassidy knows she's really gifted at working with little kids. So she decides that she'll wait until she's older to put

that gift into practice. *(Dumb teen—do it now!)*

Devon has noticed that Jesus didn't hang out with religious people all the time. Devon asked his uncle about this, and his uncle said Devon should just spend time with Christian friends so he doesn't get tempted to do stuff that wouldn't please God. But Devon thinks that what would really please God is if he became friends with a couple kids who don't know Jesus. *(Wise teen)*

Last Sunday, Martie heard the story about Jesus telling the rich guy he had to sell everything he had and give it to the poor. So this week she decided to do something kind of radical: she went online and sponsored a little kid in Columbia through Compassion International. It will take half of her babysitting money each month to follow through on this pledge. *(Wise teen—your kids will know this is the "right" answer, but if you push them a bit, they'll admit this doesn't seem very wise.)*

Of course, you can feel free to make up a few more stories of your own if you want.

HIS WORDS, MY ACTION

Pass out copies of **His Words, My Action** (Wildpage 4.1) and a pen or pencil to each student. The sheet is fairly self-explanatory. The left column is a handful of Jesus' teachings. The right column is a space to brainstorm responses.

Read through the teachings of Jesus in the left column with your students, then give them a few minutes to suggest additional teachings. Have them write a couple of these in at the blank squares.

Then ask them to take a minute, silently, to prayerfully consider the list, asking God to help them choose one they'll apply this week. After a minute, tell them to put a check mark in the square next to the one they've chosen. Encourage them to choose one that they've not been wise with—a teaching of Jesus that they've been ignoring in their life.

Then turn their attention to the second column. Ask them to take a few minutes to think of three ways they could be wise with that teaching—three ways that could put action to that teaching in their lives this week. These should be very specific action steps, including when and how they would do them. Don't let them get away with wimpy answers like, "I'll love someone this week."

Model this from your life by choosing a teaching and three action steps you've come up with for yourself. Then have several students share which teaching they've selected and what three possible wisdom steps they've come up with.

Finally, challenge your students to take this dare by choosing one of their possible action steps to carry out this week. They should check the box next to that choice.

Follow up on these choices next week (or with phone calls and e-mails throughout the week).

Be sure to close your time in prayer, thanking Jesus for the firm foundation he provides for our lives through his teachings and our relationship with him. Ask for courage and strength to follow through on these steps of wisdom. ชั

You'll Need

ชั copies of Wildpage 4.1 (**His Words, My Action,** page 44) and pens or pencils for each student

A SHORT SPONTANEOUS MELODRAMA IN THREE SILLY SCENES

Jesus Throws Down a Dare
A loose telling of Matthew 7:24-27

Characters:

Wise dude   **Dumb dude**   Rock house (1 guy)
Wind, Stream, and Rain (3 girls)   Sand house (1 guy)

Scene 1: Wise dude and dumb dude on stage.

Once there were two dudes: a wise dude and a dumb dude. The wise dude, of course, did wise things; while the dumb dude, of course, did dumb things.

One day, both of them said at the exact same time, "Hark! I have an idea!" At this point, they both massaged their own heads to get the ideas to form more fully. They rubbed their heads so hard it totally messed up their hair. Then they said, "Yes! That's it! I'll build a house!" Then they went separate ways.

Scene 2: Wise dude (standing) and Rock house (crouched, unbuilt) center stage. Stream lying on the ground next to the house. Wind and Rain waiting nearby.

The wise dude found a rock and began building his house on it. It was hard work, because he had to break away tons of rock using a sledge hammer to get the space level. The house began to take shape: at first it was just a pile of building materials. But eventually it began to look like a big strong house.

Just as the wise dude said, "It's done!" a storm hit. The Wind started to dance and swirl around the house faster and faster. The Stream rose up and splashed at the foundation of the house. And the Rain began

to beat on the house. In fact, the rain beat on the wise dude also.

But the wise dude had built his house on a strong foundation, and it stood proud, ignoring the beating rain, wind and stream.

Scene 3: Dumb dude (standing) and Sand house (crouched, unbuilt) center stage. Stream lying on the ground next to the house. Wind and Rain waiting nearby.

The dumb dude, on the other hand, got started in much the same way. But he chose a sandy beach next to the stream on which to build his house. It was easy work, and the house stood finished in no time at all. The dumb dude said, "Dude! I built a house!"

But then a storm hit! The Wind started to dance and swirl around the house faster and faster. The Stream rose up and splashed at the foundation of the house. And the Rain began to beat on the house. In fact, the fain beat on the dumb dude also. The Wind and the Stream decided the beating was a good idea, and joined in.

The dumb dude's house couldn't take it, because the sand underneath it was being washed away. Eventually, the house, along with the dumb dude, just collapsed on the ground.

The End

His Words, My Action

5.1

Here's a list of *some* of the words of Jesus. Add a few more, in your own words, at the bottom:

❏ Give to the one who asks you, and do not turn away from the one who wants to borrow from you.
❏ Love your enemies, and pray for those who persecute you.
❏ If you forgive men when they sin against you, your heavenly Father will also forgive you.
❏ You cannot serve both God and Money.
❏ Do not worry about tomorrow, for tomorrow will worry about itself.
❏ So in everything, do to others what you would have them do to you.
❏ Whoever humbles himself like this child is the greatest in the kingdom of heaven.
❏ Love your neighbor as yourself.
❏ Therefore go and make disciples of all nations.
❏ Give, and it will be given to you.
❏ Be on your guard against all kinds of greed.
❏ Whoever can be trusted with very little can also be trusted with much.
❏ Whoever lives by the truth comes into the light.
❏ My sheep listen to my voice; I know them, and they follow me.
❏ Whoever serves me must follow me; and where I am, my servant also will be.
❏ By this all men will know that you are my disciples, if you love one another.
❏ I have told you these things, so that in me you may have peace.

1.

2.

3.

After you've selected one of Jesus' teachings to be wise about, write three ways you could apply it this week:

1.

2.

3.

Now, go back and check the one you'll do!

44

Get Along!

"If your brother sins against you, go and show him his fault, just between the two of you. If he listens to you, you have won your brother over. But if he will not listen, take one or two others along, so that 'every matter may be established by the testimony of two or three witnesses.' If he refuses to listen to them, tell it to the church; and if he refuses to listen even to the church, treat him as you would a pagan or a tax collector.

"I tell you the truth, whatever you bind on earth will be bound in heaven, and whatever you loose on earth will be loosed in heaven.

"Again, I tell you that if two of you on earth agree about anything you ask for, it will be done for you by my Father in heaven. For where two or three come together in my name, there am I with them."

Then Peter came to Jesus and asked, "Lord, how many times shall I forgive my brother when he sins against me? Up to seven times?"

Jesus answered, "I tell you, not seven times, but seventy-seven times.

"Therefore, the kingdom of heaven is like a king who wanted to settle accounts with his servants. As he began the settlement, a man who owed him ten thousand talents was brought to him. Since he was not able to pay, the master ordered that he and his wife and his children and all that he had be sold to repay the debt.

"The servant fell on his knees before him. 'Be patient with me,' he begged, 'and I will pay back everything.' The servant's master took pity on him, canceled the debt and let him go.

"But when that servant went out, he found one of his fellow servants who owed him a hundred denarii. He grabbed him and began to choke him. 'Pay back what you owe me!' he demanded.

"His fellow servant fell to his knees and begged him, 'Be patient with me, and I will pay you back.'

"But he refused. Instead, he went off and had the man thrown into prison until he could pay the debt. When the other servants saw what had happened, they were greatly distressed and went and told their master everything that had happened.

"Then the master called the servant in. 'You wicked servant,' he said, 'I canceled all that debt of yours because you begged me to. Shouldn't you have had mercy on your fellow servant just as I had on you?' In anger his master turned him over to the jailers to be tortured, until he should pay back all he owed.

"This is how my heavenly Father will treat each of you unless you forgive your brother from your heart."

Matthew 18:15-35

GOALS

Students Will—

- Understand that Jesus cares about the condition of our relationships—even with people they don't get along with.
- Think about what it looks like for young teens to actively improve hurting relationships.
- Identify a couple relationships in their own life that are in bad shape, and choose a course of action to improve those relationships.

SENTENCE PARTNERSHIPS

Have students pair up. If your group is large enough, it's best if they pair up with someone they don't know very well.

Show the group this sentence: **It's difficult to get along with other people when they're jerks, or when they're different from me.** Display this sentence in a way that you can leave it up for your group to see: on a whiteboard, posterboard, overhead, or video projector.

Now tell them their challenge: they're to work for a couple minutes at saying every other word in the sentence. In other words, the first student says the first word, the second student the second word, the first student the third word, and so on. They should

You'll Need

- ॐ some way to display a sentence to your group—a white board, overhead, video projector, or posterboard.

work at it until they think they can do it fast.

After a couple minutes, have each pair face off with another pair. When you say "go," have them say the sentence, simultaneously, in the method they've prepared. The pair that gets to the word *me* first wins. The losing pair should sit down, and the winning pair should find another winning pair to compete with for the second round. Continue until you have an overall winning pair, and award them with some candy or some other small prize.

Messy Option
Bread War

If you have a highly tolerant custodial staff (is that oxymoronic?) or an outside area in which to play, consider simulating conflict with a bread war. Divide your group into two teams, and place them on two sides of a rope (or some other device to make a line down the middle). Give each team several loaves of cheap white bread (the quantity will, of course,

You'll Need
ö a buncha loaves of bread, a rope, a couple judges, and some space

depend on the size of your group—but ideally you'll have about one loaf for every four kids). Have the loaves in a pile, still in bags. Don't let anyone touch them until you say "go."

Once you say "go," the kids have 2 minutes (give or take) to get the bread on the other side of the rope. They can do this any way they want, as long as they stay on their own side. In addition, place a couple judges around the playing area; and if any student gets nailed with a sizeable piece of bread (that's where the judging comes in—they'll have to determine if it was a good solid hit with a sizeable piece, or just an errant crumb wafting through the air), they're eliminated.

Afterward, in your debrief, don't linger on who in the group is well-bred (get it?) OR who loafs when given a chance...but talk about conflict. Furious, manic, high-speed conflict—and how life's conflicts don't always involve mushy white bread.

Quick Active Option
Back-to-back

This is a quick active option that shouldn't take more than about three minutes. It could be added on to the other "Wanna Play?" intro, or you could use it instead of Sentence Partnerships if you need to

shorten your lesson time.

Have students pair up with someone. Ideally, you'd have them pair up with someone who's not their best friend—even someone they don't know (if your group is large enough to accommodate this). Have them move to an open space without chairs and sit back-to-back on the floor. Then, simply instruct them to stand up. They have to leave their hands and arms folded across their chests, and not use them at all.

Afterward, talk about how hard (or easy) it was, and how they had to work together to make it happen.

You'll Need
ö not a thing, other than a bit of space

LOTSA TRUTH

Pass out copies of **Lotsa Truth** (Wildpage 6.1, page 49) and pens or pencils (or bundles of hammers and chisels with a slab of granite if you want to use the Fred Flintstone method).

Today's truth passage is a long one! And unlike most of the other lessons in this book, it contains a bunch of truths, all loosely grouped under the concept of getting along with each other. Have students work in pairs or triplets to read the passage and then identify the truths contained in it.

The correct answers are:
- If someone hurts your feelings, go to her first; don't blab it around.

You'll Need
ö copies of Wildpage 6.1 (**Lotsa Truth,** p. 49), pens or pencils for each student, and Bibles

- Forgive people over and over again.
- If someone wrongs you, and she won't respond when you talk to her about it; take a couple of trusted people (maybe adults?,) and talk to her again.
- When you gather together with friends who know Jesus, Jesus is there with you.
- Don't be a hypocrite and expect others to forgive you when you won't forgive others.

But before you reveal the correct answers, have students offer suggestions. A few statements in the list are either true statements, or at least sound quasi-biblical, but they are not found in this passage (ooh, I'm such a sneaky monkey).

Non paper alternative: If your group is paper-challenged and regularly destroys what you hand out before reading a word of it, consider doing the above exercise as a verbal exchange. Read the passage (or have someone read it), then read the "truth statements" from the Wildpage (or project them with an overhead or PowerPoint). Have students shout out whether they think the statements are truths from the passage or not.

Ultimately, whether you go paper or paper-free, you'll need to turn the corner and get out the umbrella. Ha!—I bet that sentence completely confused you! All the truths from this passage, as stated earlier, fit loosely under the umbrella (oh, now you get it) of *"getting along with others."* Before you reveal this, ask your group if they can guess what the truths have to do with each other? **If there's one truth-statement that would summarize all of them, what might it be?**

FREEZE-FRAME ROLE-PLAYS

You've probably used role-plays before. Basically, a role-play is when you appoint characters, describe a scenario, then let the characters play out their roles, creating the dialogue as they go. To be honest, I've found these to be challenging with a large group of junior highers. A few suggestions: Role-plays work great in small groups (if your group is small already—celebrate your smallness!). If your group is large, break into small groups with a leader in each, and have each group act out the role-plays. Or, you can stay in a large group and use adult volunteers to play the roles. If you choose to use students, and you're in a large group, I strongly encourage you to choose students who are comfortable being in front of others, and who are fairly articulate and bright. Otherwise you'll end up with a kid standing in front of the group saying, "what...huh-huh...I don't know what to say...."

What makes this version of Role-Playing different is that you'll inform the actors that you'll occasionally shout out "freeze," and they'll need to freeze exactly as they are. These will be debriefing points, where you ask the audience for input. The actors will take this input into account when you tell them to resume.

Choose to freeze the action at a couple points: First, when the basic scenario is in place, freeze the action and ask your group how the characters should respond to each other if they're willing to take this dare from Jesus to get along with each other.

Later, freeze the action again (or even rewind if you think the actors did a cheesy or unrealistic job of acting the scene) to ask your group for input on where the characters should go from here.

After each role-play is finished, ask your group if it was realistic or not. If it wasn't, talk about what this would have looked like in real life, and how they could respond.

Pick and choose which role-plays to use, based on what you think would benefit your group and how much time you have.

Scene #1: Cheeseballs
Actors needed: six, in two groups of three
The set up: One group of friends is really ticked at the other group of friends because the second group has started calling them "cheeseballs." The first group doesn't know why they're doing this, but it sure bugs them!

Scene #2: Backstabber
Actors needed: Four
The set up: Two of the kids have been best friends for a long time, but one of them is hurt big-time, feeling the other one stabbed her in the back by gossiping about her. The other two actors are friends of the hurt person.

Scene #3: The Hypocrite
Actors needed: three
The set up: One student begs for forgiveness from another for telling a lie about her. But when the third

student asks forgiveness from the first for damaging a CD she'd borrowed, the first student goes ballistic.

Creative option: if your group has a good amount of time, as well as a good amount of creativity, have them create their own role-play scenarios based on a young teen application of this dare.

Don't have them script it as a drama—just create the scenario, then have them role-play it for the group.

This would also be a good small group option—to do one or two of the above role-plays in a large group, then have small groups create their own.

Whichever option you choose, be sure to discuss with the group the real truth!

Before your group meets, make copies (1/2 has many as you have kids) of **The Good Stuff Starts with Me** (Wildpage 6.2, page 50). Cut them in half along the dotted line.

Now pass them out to your students, along with a pen or pencil.

You'll Need

♂ copies of Wildpage 6.2 **(The Good Stuff Starts with Me,** p. 50) and pens or pencils for each student.

Lotsa Truth

6.1

Read today's truth passage: Matthew 18:15-35

Which of these truths are contained in this passage? (Circle the correct answers)

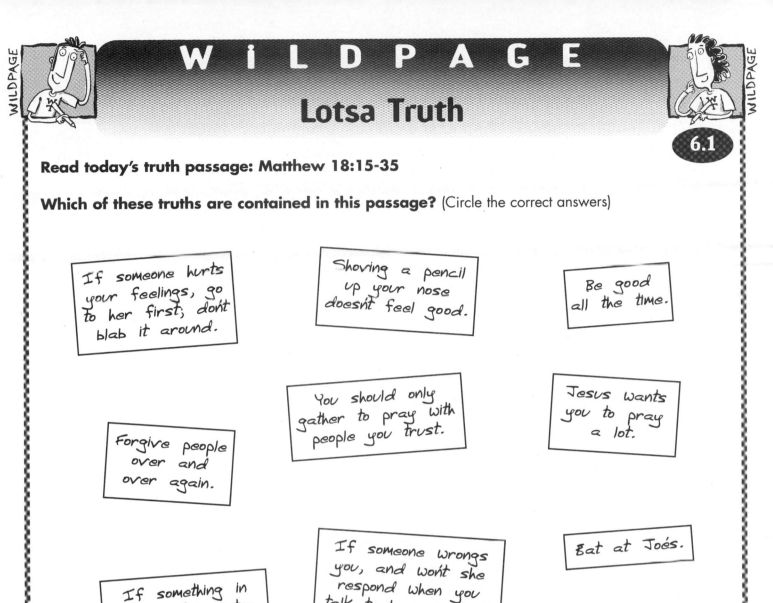

If someone hurts your feelings, go to her first; don't blab it around.

Shoving a pencil up your nose doesn't feel good.

Be good all the time.

Forgive people over and over again.

You should only gather to pray with people you trust.

Jesus wants you to pray a lot.

If something in your refrigerator looks and smells like cottage cheese but isn't, you should probably throw it away.

If someone wrongs you, and won't she respond when you talk to her about it; take a couple of trusted people (maybe adults?), and talk to her again.

Eat at Joe's.

Using Super Glue as hair gel isn't a good idea.

If someone doesn't repay you what they owe you, you should have them thrown in jail.

When you gather together with friends who know Jesus, Jesus is there with you.

Don't be a hypocrite and expect others to forgive you when you won't forgive others.

The Good Stuff Starts with Me

6.2

Honesty time! Make a list of all the people (individuals and groups of people) you don't get along with. This might include a sibling or even a parent, a handful of other students from school or your youth group, or even certain ethnic groups or cliques in your school. Try to come up with at least 6 of them:

Jesus dares you to get along with these people—to find a way, with his help, to have healthy relationships. It's a big deal to him! So look back over that list you just wrote, and choose two or three people or groups that you'll make an effort to get along with this week. Circle them. Now write here what you'll do:

- -

The Good Stuff Starts with Me

Honesty time! Make a list of all the people (individuals and groups of people) you don't get along with. This might include a sibling or even a parent, a handful of other students from school or your youth group, or even certain ethnic groups or cliques in your school. Try to come up with at least 6 of them.

Jesus dares you to get along with these people—to find a way, with his help, to have healthy relationships. It's a big deal to him! So look back over that list you just wrote, and choose two or three people or groups that you'll make an effort to get along with this week. Circle them. Now write here what you'll do:

Give Big

"Give, and it will be given to you. A good measure, pressed down, shaken together and running over, will be poured into your lap. For with the measure you use, it will be measured to you."

Luke 6:38

GOALS

Students Will—

- Hear that God promises to bless us when we give generously
- Process different ways to be generous
- Choose a gutsy act of generosity to carry out this week

YOU FIRST

This is a strange twist on the old youth group standby: the relay race. In fact, while I'll give you a suggestion, you could substitute almost any relay race into this idea to suit your needs: one that requires more or less space, one that's gross or messy, one that takes more time or less time.

The relay race I suggest is the handicap relay (I don't know, maybe this is in a book somewhere; maybe I'm making it up right here—who's to say in youth ministry?).

Divide your group into two (or more) teams. Don't tell them they're going to compete in a relay race yet. Instruct students to choose a handicap that would limit them in life in some way. Encourage them to get creative. You might suggest:

- **Blindness**
- **Only having one leg**
- **No arms**
- **Paraplegic (no use of legs)**

If your group is medium or small (30 kids or fewer), have each student quickly share his choice

You'll Need

- space to play, cones (or folding chairs) as a turning point for the relay race
- optional: a bag of candy for the winning team

with the group. If your group is larger, have the students share their choices with someone sitting near them or with their team.

Now lock in the handicaps. Announce that they cannot be changed from this point until the end of the game.

Time to start the relay! Have the teams line up on one side of your room (or outdoors if you have the time and place). Place a cone (or a trashcan or a folding chair or an 8 year-old) at some equal distance from each team line. You can have one cone per team, or just one that they all have to go around (the latter creates some fun-to-watch action!).

Their task, as a team, of course, is to run (or limp, or roll) around the cone and back to the team, tagging the next person in line who does the same. Of course, some students will have handicaps that won't limit them much. Others will have handicaps that will make it *very* difficult to even circle the cone (like a blind paraplegic girl in a Sunday dress!).

Now, just as your kids are groaning and complaining about how impossible this will be, it's time for the twist. Say something like: **Before we start, I'm going to read you a couple of verses from the Bible. This isn't an ordinary relay race, and these verses will have something to say about which team will be the winner today.**

Then read:

Matthew 20:16 ***"So the last will be first, and***

the first will be last."

Luke 6:38 *"Give, and it will be given to you. A good measure, pressed down, shaken together and running over, will be poured into your lap. For with the measure you use, it will be measured to you."*

Then begin the race! Here's where you have a very subjective role: you need to watch for the team (or members from the team—even if they don't all get it) that follow the teachings of those verses—to be generous and put others needs first. If a kid leaves his line to help someone on his own team, tell him to return to his line (you might even say: **you can't help people on your own team**). But if a kid leaves his line to help someone on another team, let him do it, and make a mental note.

The team you declare the winner at the end of the game should be the one that was slow and/or the one that helped people (even if it means cheering them on). Depending on how this shakes down, you might say something like: **Team one clearly finished first. But the members of team two *allowed* team one to finish first, and therefore, they are the winners.** Consider awarding a bag of small candy bars to the winning team.

DO THE FUNKY MATH

Make a transition by saying something like: **Okay, that seemed fairly random, didn't it? But it connects with today's dare from Jesus. If ever there was a clear DARE from Jesus, one where you can almost hear him say, "C'mon, I dare ya!" this would be it. So many things are strange to us in the way God runs the world. And in the area of giving, God's math is odd.**

Ask:
• **How many of you like math?**
• **How many don't like math?**
• **What is it about math that you like or dislike?**
• **What about story problems—do you like or dislike them more than number math?**

Give a silly example of a story problem, like: **Jeremy has 10 apples. He gives 3 to Gina, who eats them all in 3 seconds. How many apples does Jeremy have left?**

Acknowledge how simple that was, and how clear the answer should be. Even when the story problem is more difficult than that example, there's still only one correct answer—usually.

Then explain that God's math—especially when it comes to giving—is very different. Read this story problem:

Jeremy has 10 apples. He gives all 10 apples to Gina, who eats them in 10 seconds. Now Jeremy has 15 apples.

Then ask: **What seems wrong with that equation?** (allow several answers to this question.)

Time to reveal Jesus' dare. Have students look in their Bibles at Luke 6:38 (or show the passage on a screen). After they read it a couple of times, lead a discussion by asking questions like:

• **What do you think Jesus meant when he said this?**
• **What do you think Jesus meant by, "A good measure, pressed down, shaken together and running over, will be poured into your lap"?** Admittedly, this is odd language for us today. Jesus is using language people who first read the Bible would understand: he's using the language of buying and selling grain. "Pressed down and shaken together" refers to a measure of grain that's packed well, and isn't full of fluff and air.
• **Where's the dare in this verse?**
• **What, specifically, is Jesus daring us to do?**

Explain that there are very few places in the Bible where a dare comes across so plainly. Jesus is saying that his math is different when it comes to giving. When we give, we receive.

Write (or reveal) these equations one at a time, and discuss them:

X = _____
(X, of course, is the answer, in mathematics)

Don't give at all = _____
(Jesus says that if we don't give, we won't get anything in return.)

Give a little = _____
(Give a little, get little)

Give a lot = _____
(Give a lot, get even more in return!)

Now take a step backward (in your discussion, not physically!), and look at the mechanics of this process. Before your group meets, make copies of the **Funky Math** bookmarks on page 55, and cut them into strips. Now hand one out to each student in your group, and talk through the four bulleted sentences. It's impossible to be a generous giver if we're only focusing on our own needs—this is why generous giving doesn't come easily for most of us! This is especially true of young teens, who are going through one of the most significant and intimidating times of change in their lives—this naturally draws their attention almost exclusively to their own needs.

The four sentences on the bookmarks are:

- **If I'm going to be generous, I must first consider giving something.**
- **If I'm going to give, I must first notice other peoples' needs.**
- **If I'm going to notice other peoples' needs, I must first take my attention off myself.**
- **But when I *am* generous, God promises to pour grain in my lap!**

Wrap up this section by brainstorming with your group on what ways they can be generous, other than giving money.

GENEROSITY COMMERCIALS

Divide your kids into groups of 5 to 10. Use the teams that worked for the opening relay race. Or, this would be a great exercise to use in the context of small groups, if you use them (and if you aren't, what are you thinking?). Instruct the groups that they'll have about five minutes to put together a 30-second commercial for generous giving, using the stuff they've learned and talked about so far in this lesson. Their commercials can tell a story, or they can be more of a "concept commercial." But it's *very* important that they consider other forms of generous giving than just giving money (most young teens don't have much money to give, of course, but they can still practice generosity!). It would be ideal if you had an adult leader in each group to keep them on task (junior highers on task—ha!).

Give the groups five to seven minutes to create their award-winning commercials. Then pull the group back together, and have them perform their commercials. Make sure you give all attempts lots of affirmation!

Pay attention to the scope of generosity topics and applications covered by the commercials. If they seem to all focus on one area of generosity, or if they're all ideas that young teens probably can't do (like commercials where someone gives millions of dollars to someone else), make sure you continue to debrief and clarify. In this case, try to add to what's been presented, rather than diminish their efforts (if you diminish what they've done, they probably won't hear the clarification you're trying to offer, and will, instead, focus on their "failure").

GIVE IT AWAY!

Have students return to the small groups they were in to create their commercials. Ask them to take a few minutes to brainstorm together a list of ways that young teens can be generous in their giving. These should be practical—"I can do this in the next week"—ideas. If you don't have adult leaders in the groups to help direct them, you should offer categories or boundaries as guidance,.

- **How can I give money or material possessions? Who would I give to? What does it mean for me to be generous in this way?**

- **How can I give my time in a generous way?**
- **How can I give my attention to someone who needs it in a generous way?**
- **How can I give help?**
- **How about giving by using my gifts and talents?**

Then, after brainstorming, pass out pens or pencils and have them write three generosity ideas on the

You'll Need

☞ the **Funky Math** bookmarks you handed out in the last session and pens or pencils for each student.

back of their "Funky Math" bookmarks. These three ideas need to be clear—an actual plan of action. Suggest a few examples:

•This week I'll buy a sweatshirt for a homeless person, and give it to him.

•This week I'll do the dishes every night to help out my mom and dad.

•This week I'll invite a certain lonely kid from school who kinda bugs me over to my house so we can hang out together.

After they've written three ideas, have them share their work in their groups. After each student shares, have the group respond as to whether the ideas are truly generous or not, and whether they are specific enough (again, an adult leader in the groups would really help here!).

Finally, have each student choose one of her three ideas, and make a commitment to carry it out. Have students indicate this by circling that idea on their bookmarks. Again, have kids share their chosen plan of action in their groups. If your overall group isn't too large, consider having everyone share their generosity plans with the whole group. Model this by sharing one of your own!

FInally, close your time in prayer, thanking God for his funky math—for blessing us when we give. ☞

Funky Math

Luke 6:38 *"Give, and it will be given to you. A good measure, pressed down, shaken together and running over, will be poured into your lap. For with the measure you use, it will be measured to you."*

- **If I'm going to be generous, I must first consider giving something.**

- **If I'm going to give, I must first notice other peoples' needs.**

- **If I'm going to notice other peoples' needs, I must first take my attention off myself.**

- **But when I am generous, God promises to pour grain in my lap!**

Funky Math

Luke 6:38 *"Give, and it will be given to you. A good measure, pressed down, shaken together and running over, will be poured into your lap. For with the measure you use, it will be measured to you."*

- **If I'm going to be generous, I must first consider giving something.**

- **If I'm going to give, I must first notice other peoples' needs.**

- **If I'm going to notice other peoples' needs, I must first take my attention off myself.**

- **But when I am generous, God promises to pour grain in my lap!**

Funky Math

Luke 6:38 *"Give, and it will be given to you. A good measure, pressed down, shaken together and running over, will be poured into your lap. For with the measure you use, it will be measured to you."*

- **If I'm going to be generous, I must first consider giving something.**

- **If I'm going to give, I must first notice other peoples' needs.**

- **If I'm going to notice other peoples' needs, I must first take my attention off myself.**

- **But when I am generous, God promises to pour grain in my lap!**

Funky Math

Luke 6:38 *"Give, and it will be given to you. A good measure, pressed down, shaken together and running over, will be poured into your lap. For with the measure you use, it will be measured to you."*

- **If I'm going to be generous, I must first consider giving something.**

- **If I'm going to give, I must first notice other peoples' needs.**

- **If I'm going to notice other peoples' needs, I must first take my attention off myself.**

- **But when I am generous, God promises to pour grain in my lap!**

Don't Be Greedy

Then he said to them, "Watch out! Be on your guard against all kinds of greed; a man's life does not consist in the abundance of his possessions."

Luke 12:15

GOALS

Students Will—

- Understand what it means to be greedy and why Jesus wants us to be on guard against greed
- Look at ways greed shows up in the lives of young teens
- Choose a dare to move away from greed and be on guard

MINE, ALL MINE!

Spread the contents of a very large bag of small candies on the floor with your students standing around the outside in a circle. Instruct your kids that the goal of this game is to get as much candy as possible, and whoever gets the most will get a reward. Tell them that when you say "go," they can use almost any way they can think of to get as much candy for themselves: they can just grab some, they can bribe others, they can cheat and lie. The only thing they can't do is hurt someone physically.

Then release the wild animals. This could be a bit frightening to watch—like ravenous wolves going after a seal pup or something (do NOT send me complaint letters for that thought!). Anyhow, it's possible that the first round will be such mayhem that you'll need to call it a practice round, have everyone toss their cookies—I mean, toss their candy—back into the middle, and play again. Urge them to use strategy, not just frenzy.

When you've allowed enough time for a bit of after-the-initial-grab bargaining and trading, find your winner. Then announce that the winner actually gets all the candy! This will undoubtedly create cries of "that's not fair!" and "you didn't tell us that!" and "what kind of lousy youth worker are you?" Grin and bear it.

Large group variation: Duh, break into small groups, and have more than one round of this going on.

Calm option: Bring a stack of magazines, and have students tear out pictures of things they'd like to have.

Make a transition by asking something like:
- **If you could go out today and spend an unlimited amount of money on yourself, what would be the first five things you'd buy?**
- **Do you ever spend time daydreaming about all the stuff you'd like to have? Or about being rich?**
- **How do you feel about loaning out your stuff to other people?**
- **Who can define greed for me?** (Focusing on getting and keeping stuff for yourself.)

You'll Need

- large bag, or bags, of wrapped, mixed candy (you can find these in most grocery stores)—the bigger the better. You'll want to have a few individual pieces of candy for each student present.

Reader's Theater:
The Lovely Leech Sisters on the Terry Splinger Show

Before your group meets, enlist the help of five students (or adult volunteers) to be readers in a drama. They don't have to rehearse their parts or prepare—just give them enough time to read it through on their own once or twice so they don't totally stumble over the words (right, like that's not going to happen if you're using junior highers).

Place three chairs at the front of your room for the "guests" to sit in (Terry Splinger should stand like a talk show host). Before you begin the reading, make sure your group knows what a leech is (a worm-like creature that latches onto other animals—including humans—and sucks their blood).

Note to those of you pulling out pen and paper to write me a nasty note about using the word "suck" in the drama: Language is a fluid thing—meanings change. When your junior highers say, "that sucks!" it has no sexual connotations at all. I'm sure you said words your parents just didn't get.

If you don't buy into that last point... The word is used here as a play on words: Leeches suck—it's a fact of nature, even the literal implication of Proverbs 30:15.

Okay, I'm done being defensive.

After the brilliant reading is finished, reveal that this weird little piece was based on a verse from the Bible (gasp!). Have everyone turn in their Bibles to Proverbs 30:15 ("The leech has two daughters. 'Give! Give!' they cry."). After reading the verse, ask: **What do you think this verse might be saying about greed?** (This question is a major long shot, and your kids might be 100 percent clueless about how to respond—that's Okay.)

After they suggest some ideas, explain: **Leeches have a place on each end—kind of like a mouth—where they can latch on and suck. When the writer of the Proverbs talks about the leech's two daughters, it's a poetic way of referring to these two spots. But he uses the leech like a double word picture.**

First you think of the leech itself; then you think of a dad with two greedy daughters who want more all the time. And the idea is that they can never get enough. That's what greed does to us!

Now have students turn in their Bibles to the dare verse, Luke 12:15, and say something like: **Let's see what Jesus has to say about greed.** Read the passage (or have a student read it).

Ask:

- **What do you think Jesus means when he warns to "be on guard against greed?" Is it sneaky or something?** (Greed really can sneak up on us—it's easy to fall into without really thinking about it.) **What does it mean to be on guard?**

- **Why does Jesus say to "be on guard against *all kinds* of greed?" What different kinds would there be?** (Just let students brainstorm on this one. Make sure they understand that Jesus isn't only talking about money.)

- **Then Jesus says that our lives are made up of more than our possessions. What do you think that means? Why did he say that?**

- **Have you ever heard the expression, "Whoever dies with the most toys wins?" What does that mean? What would Jesus have to say about that idea?**

You'll Need

- volunteers to read the parts, copies of the **Terry Splinger Show** script (p.60) for each character; Bibles

GREEDY KIDS

Have students break into pairs or triplets, and pass out copies of **Greedy Kids** (Wildpage 8.1, page 61) and something to write with. Ask them to take a few minutes to read over the descriptions of the greedy kids and rank them from the most greedy (1) to the least greedy (5). Make sure they understand the difference between "rating" and "ranking"—they're to put these kids in order. Tell them to work together and come to agreement in their pairs or triplets about what the order should be. Don't tell your kids, but there's not "correct" ranking on these—the exercise is designed to get them thinking (and talking) about what greediness looks like in the life of a young teen. There are a couple sneaky ones in there—like Dustin, who has tons of stuff, but also likes to give it away. Greed isn't just about actually *having* stuff—it's an attitude of the heart.

After your students have had enough time to complete the sheet, debrief the exercise by asking about each character. **Is this person greedy? Why or why not? What are they greedy for? How did you rank this person, and why?**

Now make a transition to our own lives by saying something like: **Almost everyone gets greedy sometimes—that's why Jesus said we have to be on guard against it. What are other ways that people your age show greed?**

Big important question: **What does greed do to people who aren't on guard against it?** (It consumes them—just like the leech sisters, they always want more. And it becomes a distraction from focusing our lives on God.)

One more big important question: **Why does Jesus care if you're greedy or not?** It's important to make sure that these "dares" don't just become moralistic teachings about doing the right thing. Junior High kids can easily assume that Jesus just wants them to shape up and be good. This misses the point of the dares! Jesus cares about greed in our lives because he loves us, and he knows that greed hurts us.

AM I A LEACH?

Before your group meets, make copies of **Am I a Leech** (Wildpage 8.2, page 62). If you used the **Greedy Kids** exercise, your students should still have something to write with (although the writing utensil's ability to actually *write* may have become obsolete in the last 10 minutes!).

Ask your students to take a few minutes on their own to think about greed in their own lives.

You can do this two ways: Give students a few minutes on their own to fill out the whole sheet. Or, have them answer the questions one at a time and talk about each one as a group after they've filled it out (before they go on to the next question).

Close your time in prayer, thanking God for loving us so much that he wants the best for us, and asking him to help us be on guard against greed in our lives.

ꙮ

The Lovely Leech Sisters on the Terry Splinger Show
Loosely based on Proverbs 30:15

Characters:
- **Terry Splinger, talk show host**
- **Gimmie Leech, the first Leech sister**
- **Iwannit Leech, the second Leech sister**
- **Daddy Leech**
- **Studio Audience Member**

Terry Splinger: Welcome to the Terry Splinger show—we have a fantastic program tonight! Please give a big welcome to Daddy Leech and his two daughters, Gimmie and Iwannit.

<pause for applause>

Terry: Tell us a bit about yourselves.

Daddy Leech: I'm just worn out.

Terry: Why's that, Daddy Leech?

Daddy: Well, my daughters, they just suck!

Terry: That's an awful thing to say about your daughters, Daddy!

Daddy: No, I really mean it. I mean, they ARE leeches, you know?

Gimmie Leech, in a whiney voice: Daddy, can I have some more money?

Iwannit Leech, also with a whiney voice: Yeah, Dad, give us more!

Daddy: <to Terry> See what I mean? They suck. They keep begging for more and more, and they're never happy with what they have.

Terry: Well, Daddy Leech, I hate to point this out to you, but, well, you're a leech also.

Daddy: Yes, this is true. But…

Terry: And shouldn't you *assume* that your daughters suck—I mean, that's what leeches do, right?

Daddy: Yes, this is true also. It's just that they never stop!

Gimmie: What's wrong with wanting more, more, more? We just want what any sweet little leech girl wants—everything!

Iwannit: And we deserve it!

Terry: Leech daughters, will you ever get enough?

Gimmie and Iwannit: <in unison> No way!

Daddy: <sigh!>

Terry: Do we have anyone from the studio audience who'd like to ask a question?

Studio Audience Member: Yeah, I'd like to ask the Leech sisters: does it ever bother you to suck so much?

Iwannit: What do you mean? You just don't get it, do you? I mean, life is really about getting more stuff!

Gimmie: I want as much money as I can get. I want as much stuff as I can get. And I want it all to myself. If that sucks—too bad!

Terry: Well, folks, there you have it—the lovely Leech sisters, admitting they suck, and they're proud of it. Let's give our guests a hand as we say good-bye today.

Greedy Kids

Rank the following students from *Most Greedy* (1), to *Least Greedy* (5)

Camille
Camille is really a sweet girl, and she hardly ever gets into trouble. She has two little brothers, and her parents always ask her to baby-sit (and they don't pay her). Today, Camille surprised her mom by saying, "I think it's a rip-off that I have to baby-sit Timmy and Tony all the time without getting paid. I've decided that I won't do it any more unless you pay me."

Camille's greediness ranking: _____

Chase
"You can never have enough video games." That's Chase's life motto. It seems like his life revolves around finding ways to get more video games. Sure, he plays them. But what he *really* likes is getting a new one. In fact, he gets bored with them shortly after he gets a new one—the only *real* fun for him is in getting the next one.

Chase's greediness ranking: _____

Selma
Clothes are the thing for Selma. It's not that she has very many clothes. And she doesn't have enough money to buy many new things. But she's obsessed with the idea. She reads fashion magazines all the time to see what's new and to daydream about what she would look like in all the cool clothes she sees. She spends tons of time at the mall, trying on outfits she can never buy. Her goal in life is to find a way to have enough money someday, so she can buy whatever clothes she wants—closets and closets full!

Selma's greediness ranking: _____

Dustin
Dustin has what most junior highers wish they had. His parents are mega-rich, and he lives in a huge house. They buy him stuff all the time, and he has more stuff than any of his friends: CDs, gaming systems, electronic equipment (He's even got a home theater system in his bedroom!), expensive clothes. His parents have already told him he can pick whatever car he wants for his 16th birthday gift. Sometimes his parents get frustrated with Dustin, though, because he's always giving his stuff away.

Dustin's greediness ranking: _____

Cash
He always figured it made sense that his name was Cash—because nothing made him happier. He never spent his money. And he didn't trust anyone with it—even banks: so he stores all his money in secret places all over his room. He even took a bunch of money and bought gold coins, then buried them in a metal box in his backyard. None of Cash's friends have any idea that he has so much money.

Cash's greediness ranking: _____

Am i a Leech?

Rate your own greediness on this meter by adding a needle to it:

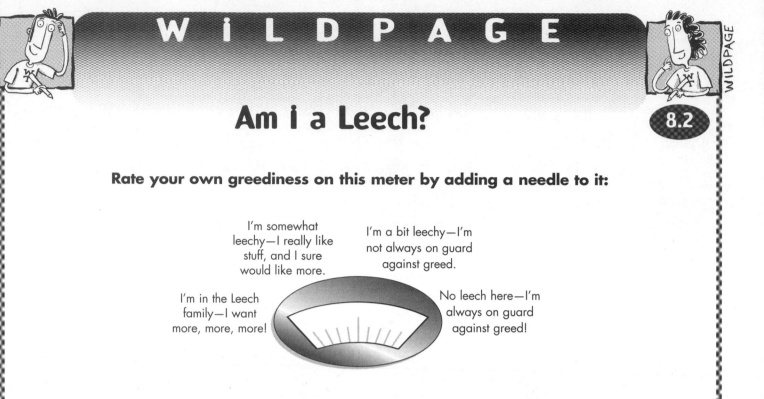

I'm somewhat leechy—I really like stuff, and I sure would like more.

I'm a bit leechy—I'm not always on guard against greed.

I'm in the Leech family—I want more, more, more!

No leech here—I'm always on guard against greed!

Write about a time when you were greedy recently:

Pick a dare:

This week I'll give something away that I really like (don't wimp out and give something away that you don't want!). What I'll give away and to whom:

This week I'll spend time every day praying that God will help me be on guard against greed. Time of day and location for this prayer:

This week I'll tell someone about the greed in my life, and ask him or her to tell me when they see me being greedy. Who I'll ask and when I'll do it:

Prove It

"Whoever can be trusted with very little can also be trusted with much, and whoever is dishonest with very little will also be dishonest with much. So if you have not been trustworthy in handling worldly wealth, who will trust you with true riches? And if you have not been trustworthy with someone else's property, who will give you property of your own?"
Luke 16:10-12

GOALS

Students Will—

- Examine what it means to be trustworthy
- Learn the benefits of being trustworthy and the pitfalls of not being trustworthy
- Understand that being consistently trustworthy isn't easy, but it's possible to do with God's help

CAN THIS PERSON BE TRUSTED?

You'll Need

- a variety of pictures of individual people, large enough for kids to see (this would be ideally done using MediaShout or PowerPoint and a video projector)
- some way to display the pictures for everyone to see
- pencils or pens
- paper

Before your students gather for this lesson, you need to gather some pictures. They can be pictures of celebrities, politicians (local and national), church staff members, area school faculty members, youth group volunteers (who can be disguised, just for fun), some of the kids' parents—you get the idea! It would also be good to include pictures of people they don't know as well, obscure magazine ad models, old yearbook pictures, random people you see on the street.

If you have access to the necessary technology, scan the pictures, and make a PowerPoint slide or MediaShout cue to show them (or easier yet, just choose pictures off the internet so you don't have to scan them!). If not, post the pictures somewhere for all the students to see, and number the pictures.

If you're using the PowerPoint method, have the students sit and then pass out pieces of paper and something to write with. Ask the students to number their papers one through however many pictures you have to use. Explain to the kids that you're going to show them some pictures of people, and they should rate each person on a scale of one to 10 (you may wish to include the rating scale on each slide so you don't have to remind them every time you change pictures). One is "I don't trust them as far as I can throw them!" and 10 is "I trust them like I trust my own grandmother." Then begin the slide show. You may have to run through the slides a time or two to give them a chance to make their ratings.

If you're using the bulletin board method, hang it somewhere in your room where kids can gather around it freely. As the kids enter your youth room, have a volunteer hand them a piece of paper and something to write with, directing them to the bulletin board to make their ratings before the meeting begins.

And if you don't have time to find pictures, much less scan them into a fancy presentation, just use names of people (real and fictional) like Bill Gates, Osama bin Laden, Harry Potter, Brittney Spears, Pink, George W. Bush, and so on (of course, these names made sense at the time I'm writing this – so choose your own if they don't make sense anymore—some of you are already saying, "Is Pink a person or a color?"). And if you want a more active option, make one wall represent "1", and the opposing wall represent "10" and have students move somewhere in-between the two walls to register their responses.

Once the students finish making their ratings, go through the pictures or names again and ask for a show of hands as to who rated each one with a 10, a 9, and so on. Ask for some reasons why the students rated each person high or low. Pay close attention to the reasons the kids give for the how they rated the people they don't know personally. (For example, was it only because of the person's appearance? Was it because of something their parents have said about a certain politician?)

Optional Idea
To Tell the Truth

If you're familiar with the old game show *To Tell the Truth*, (You gotta be as old as me to remember, unless you're a Game Show Network junkie!) you may want to begin your lesson with a round or two of that

instead. Determine how many rounds you want to play, then think of an unusual hobby or experience that an adult leader or student has that most students don't know about—been sky-diving, used to break-dance, ate a grasshopper, whatever. Contact the appropriate people who have these pursuits before the group meets and ask them if they'd be willing to participate. If so, ask them to provide a written description of their unusual hobby or experience for the two other volunteers who will pretend to have been skydiving or eaten grasshoppers or whatever during their round. Whatever details they can give to the two pretenders will add realism to the responses, add some difficulty to the game, and will help you make your big point later on.

Once your volunteers are ready to go, set up the game for the students. Explain that the three people sitting up front all claim to be break-dancers (for the sake of an example), but only one of them has really done this. Tell the students they're allowed to ask the panelists questions to try to determine which one is the real break-dancer. It is crucial that your panelist volunteers be able to keep a straight face while lying! Otherwise the game will end too soon for you to

You'll Need
- adult or student actors
- descriptions of a hobby or career

demonstrate anything helpful.

Limit the questions to about seven per round. Students may ask only one question during a round, but they should pay attention to the other questions that are asked (so there aren't any repeats) and the answers that are given. The questions don't have to be yes-or-no format—they can ask anything they like.

When the group has used up all seven questions, ask them to vote for the panelist they believe is the real break-dancer by a show of hands or applause. After they've voted say: **Will the real break-dancer please stand up?** Have all your panelists start to stand up and look at each other, then the two impostors should sit down while the real boogaloo remains standing.

After each round ask the students to share why they chose the panelist they did. What made them believe the person they voted for was being honest about their hobby or experience? Why did they doubt that the others' testimonies were true?

WE'RE ONLY HUMAN

Begin this next part by asking a few questions to gauge your students' understanding of what it means to be trustworthy—

- **Who can define the word *trustworthy*? What does it mean?**
- **What are some characteristics of a trustworthy person?**
- **Do you believe people are more or less trustworthy today than they were 2000 years ago? 200 years ago? 20 years ago? 5 years ago?** (Ask students to explain why they feel this way.)

You'll Need
- copies of **Whom Can We Trust?** Wildpage 9.1 (p. 67), pens or pencils, Bibles.

Explain that some great stories in the Bible describe breaks in trust between family members, between leaders and the people they're supposed to lead, and between strangers.

Divide the students into smaller groups or clumps, each with an adult leader if possible. Hand out copies of **Whom Can We Trust?** Wildpage 9.1 (page 67), one to each group, and something to write with.

Assign one of the following passages to a different small group to read and discuss (using the questions on the Wildpage as a guide).

- **Genesis 4:3-16** (Cain versus Abel; God trusted Cain to offer his best, but instead he killed his brother in a fit of sibling rivalry.)
- **Exodus 32** (Moses trusted Aaron to keep an eye on the Israelites while he was off talking to God. Instead, Aaron collects gold to make an idol for the people to worship in their boredom, and then he claims the golden calf magically appeared while Moses was away.)
- **2 Samuel 11:1-17; 12:1-10** (The Israelites trusted David to lead them justly. But after succumbing to lust and adultery, he arranged for Uriah's death to ease his guilt.)
- **Acts 5:1-11** (Members of the early church trusted Ananias and Sapphira to honestly give whatever they could for the benefit of all believers. But this couple learned the hard way that you can't fool God.)

After the groups have time to read and talk about their passage, they should create a one- to two-minute commercial for an episode of *Trust Tower*. Introduce it to the groups as a "weird reality show where people (typically close friends or family members) are trapped together in a tiny room at the top of a tall tower where they can really be honest—and have opportunity to let each other down. As the losers are confronted with their acts of betrayal (similar to the way God confronted Cain, Nathan confronted David, Moses confronted Aaron, and Peter confronted Ananias and Sapphira). They're forced to climb down the outside of the tower using only a rope made of horsehair. And it's all captured on live television!"

Each small group should prepare to perform their *Trust Tower* commercial for the rest of the youth group. And the adult leaders should make sure each group's commercial includes enough information about the Bible story so the rest of the group gets the gist of what took place in each case. Every commercial should begin with the phrase, "Don't miss next week's episode full of betrayal on *Trust Tower* when…". (Note: If your group of students is typical junior highers, ask the adult leaders to serve as facilitators and give the larger group some clues as to which passage their group acted out and the basic gist of what took place. Think of them as serving a host role, like Jeff Probst on *Survivor*.)

To wrap up this section, ask the groups to share examples of both "worldly wealth" and "true riches" that they listed for qthe last question on the **Whom Can We Trust?** Wildpage.

Now say something like: **We've spent some time looking at what it means to be trustworthy and looking at some great examples of untrustworthy behavior. But how trustworthy are you? Can your family trust you? Your friends? How about your teachers and coaches at school? The leaders in our church and youth group? Can strangers trust you? Is there a difference in how trustworthy you are when you're with different groups of people—say, between how you are at church and at school? Home and sports practice? At the mall or movie theater and at a friend's house?** Explain that you've got a pop quiz that will help determine their T.Q. or "trustworthiness quotient."

Hand out copies of **Can I Be Trusted?** Wildpage 9.2 (pages 68-69) and something to write with to each student. Warn them that they should answer as honestly as they can—if they answer as though they're perfectly trustworthy 24/7, then that's a sure sign of untrustworthiness!

Give them about 5 minutes to complete the quiz. It

You'll Need

- copies of **Can I Be Trusted?** Wildpage 9.2 (pp. 68-69), pens or pencils would probably keep everyone on task more if you read the questions out loud and have them fill in their answers as you go. Then have them trade papers with someone they trust and grade each other's quizzes. This quiz doesn't have any right and wrong answers. However, if a student has a lot of E (too good to be true) answers, they may not be very trustworthy.

The students should look over their partner's answers and then rate how trustworthy they feel that person is on the same 1 to 10 scale from the beginning of the meeting— 1 is "I don't trust them as far as I can throw them!" and 10 is "I trust them like I trust my own grandmother." Ask them to return the quiz to its owner, and then discuss the results. Ask if anyone is surprised by the rating received.

DO THE RIGHT THING

Ask students to take another look at their T.Q. quizzes. Give them a few minutes to consider each scenario described in questions 1 through 10 and choose the top three areas mentioned in these questions that they need to improve (gossip, cheating, borrowing from others, obeying parents).

They should place a star next to their three choices.

Now push them a little harder, and ask them to pick one specific area that they're going to work on this week to be a more trustworthy person. Ask them to put a box around the question that represents the area they plan to work on. Have them share their choices with their quiz partner to help them be accountable to their choice.

End with a time of prayer for your students. Ask God to remind them that being trustworthy is more than being honest, it's being responsible, following through, caring for others, showing loyalty,

You'll Need

🐦 copies of **Can I be Trusted?** Wildpage 9.2 (pp. 68-69), pens or pencils

and much more. Pray that the students will find ways to prove their trustworthiness to others—friends and strangers alike—in the days to follow. 🐦

Once your students have a clear picture of their own level of trustworthiness, challenge them to do better in the areas where they're lacking. Use a Polaroid or digital camera to take a picture of each student.

If you use a Polaroid camera, write the following across the bottom of the picture, "Am I trustworthy?" or "Can you trust this face?" (To save time, before the meeting begins, print out these statements on mailing labels or stickers so the students can stick them onto their pictures.) If you use a digital camera, you can add this text to the picture before printing them out for the students. You may wish to take the kids' pictures at the beginning of the meeting and then ask someone to create and add the text to each photo and print them out so they're ready by the end of the lesson.

Before the students leave, replace the pictures you posted on the bulletin board for the first activity with the pictures of your students. They can either take the pictures home with them to display on their dresser or bathroom mirror as a reminder of how they need to act in trustworthy ways, or you can leave the photo display up in your youth room to remind them at the beginning of next week's meeting that outward appearances aren't as important as inward character.

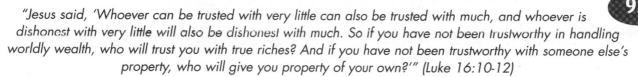

Whom Can We Trust?

9.1

"Jesus said, 'Whoever can be trusted with very little can also be trusted with much, and whoever is dishonest with very little will also be dishonest with much. So if you have not been trustworthy in handling worldly wealth, who will trust you with true riches? And if you have not been trustworthy with someone else's property, who will give you property of your own?'" (Luke 16:10-12)

Assigned Scripture Passage _____

Look up your assigned Scripture passage, and answer the following discussion questions.

1. Who are the characters in this story?

2. Summarize the passage with a just a couple of sentences that describe what took place.

3. Who was the betrayer in this passage?

4. What had the betrayer been entrusted to do? In your opinion was this person entrusted with "very little" or with "much"? (see Luke 16:10)

5. What was the relationship between the betrayed and the betrayer in this passage?

6. Name at least one consequence of this betrayal (for the betrayer as well as anyone else in the story).

7. Referring to Luke 16:10-12, what are some examples of "worldly wealth"? What are some examples of "true riches"?

Can i Be Trusted?

_____ **1. I return library books** _____
a. never.
b. sometimes a week or two late, but I always pay the fine.
c. a day late most of the time.
d. when they're due or even a little early.
e. the day after I check them out, just to be sure they're back on time.

_____ **2. When my parents ask me to do my chores, I** _____
a. pretend I can't hear them talking to me and wait until they're so frustrated that they do my chores for me.
b. say I will, but then I don't start doing them until they've nagged me 100 more times.
c. pay my little brother or sister to do them.
d. do them right away.
e. always do them before they have to ask me.

_____ **3. In the past when I've borrowed things from a friend,** _____
a. I've just kept it and pretended it was mine!
b. I've returned something that was damaged while I had it, but I told my friend it was like that when I borrowed it.
c. I've lost what I borrowed, but I always paid them back.
d. I've taken really good care of it and returned it before they asked me to.
e. I never borrow things from others.

_____ **4. When I hear a good piece of juicy gossip about somebody, I** _____
a. share it at my lunch table or in homeroom, wherever I have the biggest audience.
b. call my best friend and make them promise not to tell anybody else.
c. believe it's true, but I don't tell anybody else.
d. don't pass it on. Gossip only hurts people.
e. talk to the person that the gossip is about and try to set the record straight.

_____ **5. If I'm taking a test or quiz and happen to notice that I can totally see the paper of the smart guy sitting in front of me, I** _____
a. copy down all of his answers and motion to my best friend sitting next to him that she should copy off him as well.
b. copy down all of his answers.
c. only look at the answers for the really tough questions.
d. keep my eyes on my own paper.
e. ask the teacher to move him so I won't be tempted to cheat.

_____ **6. If someone approaches me to ask for directions, I** _____

    a. tell them the wrong way to go, just for a good laugh.

    b. pretend I don't know how to get there when I do know.

    c. tell them a really roundabout way to get there. They'll get where they need to be eventually!

    d. tell them where they need to go.

    e. take them where they want to go, if it's not too far out of my way.

_____ **7. If my youth pastor asked me to help lead a mission trip, I would** _____

    a. say I'm busy during that time even though I'm not.

    b. agree to go, but then call in sick the day before the trip.

    c. say I don't want to go.

    d. agree to go and follow through on my promise.

    e. go and recruit people to join me.

_____ **8. If my friends and I are doing something we're not supposed to do (skateboarding in the mall, messing around instead of being in class, hanging out past curfew, and so on) but they get caught and I don't, I** _____

    a. tell on another friend who also wasn't caught, just to take the heat off of me.

    b. ask some other friends to lie and say I was with them at the time.

    c. find some new friends and pretend I don't know those other rule-breakers.

    d. keep quiet and beg my friends not to rat on me.

    e. confess to the crime even though I could have gotten away with it.

_____ **9. If my coach told me to run laps after practice for messing around but then leaves me and doesn't watch, I would** _____

    a. sit down and wait a little bit before running one really fast lap and heading into the shower.

    b. run half of the laps and then head to the showers.

    c. walk the required number of laps and start running if I see Coach coming.

    d. run the laps I'm supposed to run, then apologize to the coach for messing up.

    e. run my laps plus 10 more to teach myself a lesson.

_____ **10. When my best friend confides in me, I** _____

    a. sometimes let it slip to some other friends at school, but I never let my friend know.

    b. can't help myself! I tell my cousin, but he lives in another state so that doesn't count.

    c. try to keep it a secret, but if I don't then I always apologize afterward.

    d. keep what she says to myself and don't even tell my parents.

    e. ask her not to tell me things they don't want me to tell others. I just can't keep a secret!

Live in the Light

"Everyone who does evil hates the light, and will not come into the light for fear that his deeds will be exposed. But whoever lives by the truth comes into the light, so that it may be seen plainly that what he has done has been done through God."

John 3:20-21

GOALS

Students Will—

- Understand the abstract biblical concept of light equaling truth
- Speculate about what it looks like for a young teen to live in the light
- Choose an area in their own lives where they've been living in darkness, and make a commitment to move into the light

Open with this-should-be-obvious comment: When we use metaphors in our common language, they can always be taken too far. This is even true of biblical metaphors. In the case of biblical imagery of light and dark, some idiots throughout time have used this as a basis for racial prejudice, as if the Bible were in some way commenting on skin color. Of course, this is absurd. But it is possible that some of your students will either wonder about this or have heard this idea. Be especially sensitive to darker-skinned students in your group. If there's any question, make the truth extremely clear (come into the light!).

WANNA PLAY?

IN THE DARK!

Distribute copies of **In the Dark!** (Wildpage 10.1, page 75) and pens or pencils to each student. Tell them they're going to compete in a little game highlighting things we do I the dark (yeah, you might get a snicker or two from a sex-obsessed kid—just roll with it). The first person to fill in all the blanks with initials wins.

They can only get someone's initials one time (unless your group is smaller than the number of spaces). And they can do the items in any order they want.

Say "go" and watch the bedlam proceed—unless you have one of those groups that refuses to participate in stuff like this, then when you say "go" you'll watch the hesitation begin.

After a few kids have reached you with completed forms (quickly glance them over to verify that they have actual initials in the blanks, and not repeats), call an end to the game. Consider awarding a small candy prize to the winner—or the first three finished.

Make a transition to your teaching time by asking:

• **Assuming you're not asleep, what things does darkness to do your life?** Darkness (or lack of light) makes it hard to see, makes it hard to find your way, makes it difficult to discern reality (yeah, like any kid's going to say that last one!).

• **Pretend you're walking in the dark in a room or area you've never been in before.**

You'll Need

- copies of **In the Dark!** (Wildpage 10.1, p.71), and pens or pencils for each squirrel… I mean, student
- optional: a small candy prize for the winner.

There's no light at all, and you have to feel your way. Then someone turns on a light. What differences does this make? Duh—you can see! The light increases your knowledge because you can now see obstacles you didn't know about before. And the light increases your movement, because you don't have to move with hesitation anymore.

Active (and time-consuming) option:
Sardines

This is a classic youth ministry game, and it will set up your topic for today swimmingly (there's a word you don't see too often!). "Sardines" is basically hide-and-seek in reverse, in that the everyone tries to find the person who's "it," rather than the other way around.

Clearly define the boundaries of the playing area for your group before you begin. Playing this inside a darkened church is just a kick (of course, it's also best if there aren't other groups meeting in the church, or they'll get pretty hacked when you turn off all the lights on them!). Of course, if you're limited to a portion of your church, it can still work, as long as there are good places to hide.

Choose a student (or pair of students) to be "it." This person goes off from the group and hides somewhere. Give him about 3 minutes to get settled. Then release the hounds! The rest of the group is to prowl around, trying to find the one in hiding. Don't allow them to walk around in anything larger than a group of two or three. Large packs of kids roaming around will kill the game. And here's the twist: when someone finds the hider, they join him! If you group has more than a few kids in it, this will become increasingly difficult as more and more people find the hidden gaggle. Eventually, one person (or one pair of kids) will be the last to find the now-overflowing pile of sardines, and is "it" for the next round.

This is an ideal game for a group of 12 to 25, but it works with any size (I've even played it with 200—which was a total riot).

You'll Need

ᵔ space (either multiple rooms or a large outdoor space with places to hide), darkness (either by dimming lights or by the fact that you're outside and it's nighttime!)

As you work through this lesson, the point of using this game should be obvious to you (don't count on it being obvious to your kids—the only thing obvious to them is that your teaching time is "probably about God"). The connection is this: darkness hides stuff; light reveals things. Duh!

LIGHT PASSAGES

Tell your students that the Bible mentioned light over 200 times! That's a lot of light! If you have a fairly biblically literate group (this wouldn't be my group—the kids in my church don't know Paul from Pilate; the other day I asked how many had, out of 100, had heard of Zacchaeus? Three had!), ask them to think of some "light verses"—or, if that's too hard, some different ways that the Bible uses the word "light." If they're fairly Bible-clueless (or really, this would be good to say to any group of young teens), explain that the Bible was written to a group of people—originally—who loved to use word-pictures. And the writers of the Bible use the word light to describe lots of things besides the opposite of darkness. Often, light means "truth." That's the meaning we're going to look at today.

You'll Need

ᵔ copies of **Light Passages** Wildpage 10.2 (p 76), pens or pencils for each student, Bibles.

Now distribute copies of **Light Passages** (Wildpage 10.2, page 76) and pens or pencils to each student. Of course, if you used the opening activity handout, they'll already have pens or pencils, with which (by now) they've done a combined total of approximately $4000 damage to your church. Have students work in pairs or triplets to choose the real passages. The correct answers are:
1. *Genesis 1:3-4*
2. *2 Samuel 22:29*
4. *Job 28:11*

6. *Psalm 43:3*
7. *Psalm 119:105*
8. *Matthew 5:14-16*
11. *John 3:20-21*
12. *Ephesians 5:8*

The "no handout, my kids will shred them" option: This would be a VERY easy exercise to convert to a PowerPoint or MediaShout presentation (or even overhead transparencies if you're in some kind of a time warp and still livie in the mid-'80s!). You could play it as a game of sorts with pairs or triplets deciding whether each verse is real or not. Heck, you could even award points and give out a gold star to the kid with the most accurate Bible knowledge (or maybe not).

Either way (handout or no handout), unpack the exercise by asking this list of questions:

- **How is light like truth?** Ooh, this is going for the jugular right from the start! The basic idea (which *of course* I don't need to explain to *you*) is that light exposes reality and darkness hides reality. In that way, light is a metaphor for truth.

- **A couple verses talk about God turning our darkness into light. What's that mean?** God brings us out of lies and into truth.

- **A couple more talk about God's light guiding us. How does that work; what does that look like?** God's truth guides us, and brings us to more truth.

- **One verse said, "Everyone who does evil hates the light" and "whoever lives by the truth comes into the light." What do you think those mean?** Since evil is all about untruth, those who pursue evil aren't interested in truth.

- **What does it mean to be "Children of Light?"** Christ followers committed to truth!

Of course, you can feel free to add your own questions to this list.

IN THE LIGHT?

Before your group meets, make two signs: one that says IN THE LIGHT and one that says NOT IN THE LIGHT. Tape them up on opposite walls in your room. Ideally, this will be in an area where kids have the ability to move back and forth toward one or the other without climbing over rows of chairs or other hurdles (like maybe the custodial supplies, if your junior high meeting room as near the bottom of the pecking order as in many churches).

Have all of your students stand, and tell them they are to be the points on a continuum. Point out the two signs, and explain that the space between the two extremes can mean "kinda in the light" or "pretty much in the light" depending on where they stand in relation to the two signs.

Now read the following mini case studies. After each one, ask your students to move somewhere on the continuum to show how much that young teen is taking this dare from Jesus. You may have to encourage them (over and over and over again) that they can think for themselves, and they don't have to stand next to their friends.

> **You'll Need**
>
> ☼ one sign that says IN THE LIGHT and one that says NOT IN THE LIGHT taped to opposite walls.

- **Marissa has been cheating in her Spanish class all semester. But she's decided to come into the light and stop.**

- **Tanner's mom wants him to say she's not home when her office calls. But he's totally not comfortable doing this, and he tells his mom he won't lie for her.**

- **Corin** wants to tell Jen the truth, that she told Jen's secret. But she knows it will really hurt Jen. So Corin decides it's better for Jen if she just keeps it to herself.

- **Tommy** has been running from the truth for a long time: he knows God is real, but he's afraid that if he becomes a Christian, God will mess up his life. But Tommy decides to give God a chance.

- **Rochelle** doesn't know whether to believe her brother or her sister. They're telling her different stories about why her parents got divorced, and they are both saying the other one is lying. So Rochelle decides to pray that God will make the truth clear to her.

- **Anton** turns on lights all over his house all the time and never turns them off. It really bugs his mom, who complains about the electricity bill. But Anton always says, "I like living in light."

- **Bethany** took a huge risk today: she told all her friends that she wouldn't be involved in their gossip anymore. She'll probably get left out of stuff now, but she felt it was an important thing for her to do.

- **Dillon** always believed that his church was right on everything it believes about God. But lately he's been struggling with the fact that so many Jesus followers believe different things. So he's decided to read the Bible and try to understand different things about his faith.

- **Maddie** didn't do her homework. And now her teacher is asking her if she did. She wants to tell the truth, but she really needs a good grade in this class. She's thinking about telling a little white lie about why she didn't get it done.

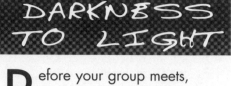

DARKNESS TO LIGHT

Before your group meets, make copies of **Darkness to Light** (Wildpage 10.3, page 77), and cut them in half. Pass them out to your students, along with a pen or pencil.

Then say something like:
Take a minute to think about some area in your life where you've been struggling to come into the light (truth). Maybe there's a lie you tell all the time. Maybe you're struggling with a certain sin, but you won't admit it.

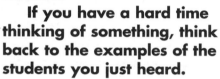

You'll Need

ᴖ copies of **Darkness to Light** Wildpage 10.3 (p. 77), pens or pencils for each student.

If you have a hard time thinking of something, think back to the examples of the students you just heard.

Now ask them to describe the way they're living in the dark by writing a phrase or sentence in the dark box. Sure, what they write won't really show up! That's okay—it will give them more freedom to write honestly (and raise their interest in the exercise).

Then have them write a specific action step they can take to move into the light in that area of their lives, in the empty (lit) box. After they've had a chance to write something, challenge them to sign the paper as a commitment to follow through with this dare.

Make sure you close your time in prayer, thanking God for being committed to truth in our lives; thanking God for the fact that we can always believe what he says since he's so committed to truth; and asking God for courage to step into the light. ᴖ

In the Dark!

Get initials for each of these items to prove you've completed them. You can't get the same person's initials more than once. You can complete these in any order you wish.

Nap Time!

Lay down on the floor, and close your eyes for 15 whole seconds (count them!). Then have someone who saw you initial here: _____

At the Movies

Get two more people, and arrange your chairs like you're in a movie theater. Pretend you're watching a movie. Eat pretend popcorn. Say, "Ooh! Ah!" Then laugh together, long and hard, pointing at the imaginary movie screen. Have both of your fellow movie watchers initial here: _____ _____

Stargazer

Get with someone, and pretend you're looking through a telescope at stars in the sky. Take turns looking. Point at the sky and make up names for stars. After about 30 seconds, have that person initial here: _____

Night Raid

Get with two other people, and pretend you're on a night commando raid into enemy territory. Sneak around and watch out for snipers. After successfully reaching your destination (really, after about a minute), have them both initial here: _____ _____

75

Light Passages

10.2

Which of these verses about light are actually in the Bible?
Check the ones you think are real.

❏ 1. And God said, "Let there be light," and there was light. God saw that the light was good, and he separated the light from the darkness.

❏ 2. You are my lamp, O LORD; the LORD turns my darkness into light.

❏ 3. Light comes from the Lord, and it is a good thing.

❏ 4. He searches the sources of the rivers and brings hidden things to light.

❏ 5. He turned on the light in the room, and said, "Thank you, God, for this light."

❏ 6. Send forth your light and your truth, let them guide me.

❏ 7. Your word is a lamp to my feet and a light for my path.

❏ 8. You are the light of the world. A city on a hill cannot be hidden. Neither do people light a lamp and put it under a bowl. Instead they put it on its stand, and it gives light to everyone in the house. In the same way, let your light shine before men, that they may see your good deeds and praise your Father in heaven.

❏ 9. The light that is lighter than all other lights is the light that was once known as the light, and is now and forever more the light.

❏ 10. God so loved the light that he gave his only begotten light, that whosoever believed in the light, will have eternal light.

❏ 11. Everyone who does evil hates the light, and will not come into the light for fear that his deeds will be exposed. But whoever lives by the truth comes into the light, so that it may be seen plainly that what he has done has been done through God.

❏ 12. For you were once darkness, but now you are light in the Lord. Live as children of light.

Darkness to Light

Where I've been

Where I'm going

_____
Signature

Know You're His

"My sheep listen to my voice; I know them, and they follow me. I give them eternal life, and they shall never perish; no one can snatch them out of my hand."

John 10:27-28

GOALS

Students Will—

- Think about what it means to have security in Christ
- Talk about examples of students who aren't living with this understanding
- Write a prayer to God that expresses thanks for the security we have in him

BREAK OUT

Have your students cluster into groups of about seven to ten. Yeah, I know—for some of you that's your whole group. No worries: so you have one cluster! Choose someone from each cluster to stand in the middle of the circle. It would be swell if this person(s) was one of the smaller people in the group. But don't make a big show of choosing the smallest kid (they're usually self-conscious enough about being small).

Now have the rest of the students in each circle tighten up, interlock arms, and try to make an impenetrable barrier. When you say "go," the student(s) in the middle should try to get outside the group.

Watch to make sure this doesn't get violent! Last thing you need is a boy in the middle trying to prove he's tough enough by taking out the knees of a 6th grade girl.

Most kids will eventually be able to get out (some girls who are more interested in being captured than released will have a difficult time). You can play as many rounds as you'd like, putting a different kid in the middle each time.

You'll Need

- absolutely positively nuthin'! ('cept a little bit o' space)

After the game, ask this series of questions:

- **How difficult was it to break out of the circle?**
- **Have you ever been trapped in a building or room that you couldn't get out of? What happened?**
- **When is it good to be stuck in something?**
- **When is it bad to be stuck in something?**

WRITTEN FOR TODAY

The dare in this lesson is one of those biblical passages dripping with wonderful Middle-Eastern animal imagery. Problem is, most people teaching these lessons don't live in the Middle East. And few even work with kids who are familiar with animals other than cats, dogs, hamsters and the occasional rat. All that to say: the nuances of a passage can be missed if we don't stop to unpack them.

You'll Need

- one copy of **Written For Today** Wildpage 11.1 (p. 83), and a pen or pencil for every other student

So once in a while, I like to have junior highers re-word passages as if they were written today. Some of you will enjoy this process with your students. Others of you might get a bit twitchy at the thought of rewriting scripture ("Doesn't it say somewhere that I'll

go straight to hell, or at least to Detroit, if I change one jot or tittle?") Well, my most compassionate and gentle response is: lighten up. You and your students won't actually be "changing scripture," but rather, interpreting it. Think of this exercise as writing a commentary!

Okay, enough of that.

Here's whatcha do: have students work in pairs or triplets (they'll be able to accomplish this easier if they work together than if they work on their own—plus it will make it feel less like school work). Give each pair or triplet something to write with, along with a half-sheet copy of **Written For Today** (Wildpage 11.1). The assignment is fairly self-explanatory: they should take a couple minutes to think of a different way to write the passage as if it had been written to junior highers today.

While they're working, make sure you circulate around the room to check that they understand what you've asked them to do (and verifying that they're not using the time to write crude poems or odes to monster trucks).

After a few minutes, have several students share their work. Be sure to encourage all efforts that aren't attempts to distract. Then ask these questions:

• **It's one thing for Jesus to say that we should follow him. But what's He mean when He says, "I know my sheep?"** *It's an amazing thing that Jesus knows us—inside and out. This passage is not primarily about obedience, but about belonging. Jesus knows us because we belong to Him!*

• **The most important part of that verse for our dare today is the last sentence: no one can snatch them out of my hand. What does that mean?** *Again, since we **belong** to Jesus, no one can take us away from him.*

• **This is a tough one—can you find the dare in this passage?** *This dare is very different from most of them. Most of the dares in these lessons are action-oriented. This dare is knowledge-oriented. Jesus is daring us to know that we're totally his—that we're totally safe in him, and that nothing or no one can take us away from him.*

• **What things in life can you be totally, 100 percent sure about?** *Allow kids to make suggestions if they want, but the reality is, we can be totally sure about very few things .*

• **Is there something in this passage that Jesus is saying we can be totally sure about?** *Yes, he's saying we can be totally confident in belonging to him. No sin on our part can take us away from him. This is a very important truth for junior highers to understand.*

• **So what's the dare again?** *Depending on the maturity of your group, this may be next to impossible for them to answer—even if you've already covered it in the questions above. Jesus dares us to trust that we are totally his, and that there's nothing we can do to get him to let go of us.*

Case study time! I love using case studies with young teens because they help bridge the gap from abstract to concrete and back again. Understanding this security stuff is pretty abstract. But using stories of young teens will help your students get it.

Use the following three stories (read 'em) to lead a discussion on this security dare. After you read each story, have students suggest different responses. Make sure you get more than one response for each question—and ideally, not all from the same overeager kid (yeah, most of us have one of those kids)!

• **Charlotte is freaked. She's been a Jesus follower for a long time—since she was a little kid. And all that time, she's been pretty good about doing what she thinks Jesus wants her to do. But last week she made a really stupid choice. She went to a party with a friend, and she decided to have a drink. It was some kind of alcohol—really sweet and tasty—and she decided to have another. And then another. At some point, Charlotte realized she was drunk! She couldn't even believe it. The next day she felt *so* guilty—and ever since then, she's sure Jesus has no use for her any more. She doesn't even know if she can call herself a Christian anymore. If Charlotte told you this story, what would you say to her?**

This case study gets at the common thought teenagers have that if they commit some big-time sin, God won't want them anymore.

You'll Need

ö Not a single thing—you're welcome.

• **Chaz has it all figured out. He heard his pastor preach a sermon about how Jesus will never let go of him. Chaz thought about that a lot. And he decided that it no longer mattered if he sinned. He knew Jesus didn't really like it and all—but he figured he was secure in Jesus, so his behavior didn't really matter all that much. What would you say to Chaz if he told you this?**

This case study deals with the thought that may have already arisen for a few of your kids: if I have security, why don't I just sin all the time? Help your students understand that while Jesus still loves us and won't leave us, our sins have natural results that he won't remove us from. And this kind of attitude is really like slapping Jesus in the face—not the kind of behavior that makes sense in a relationship.

• **Caydie has been in your church as long as you can remember—you were both little kids there together and have grown up together. And *every* time there's a chance to become a Christian, Caydie responds. Every summer at camp, Caydie "becomes a Christian" again. Every time there's a special speaker at a youth event, Caydie wants to become a Christian again. She's probably "become a Christian" about 100 times, as far as you can tell. Caydie told you she keeps doing it over and over again because she just wants to be sure. What would you say to Caydie?**

This case study brings out a behavior that's common for some young teens. They feel like they have to make a new decision for Christ every time there's a chance. And in a sense, they're right: we do need to choose Christ every day—or even more often! But we don't need to "become a Christian" again, as if we'd lost our salvation in the meantime. Help kids understand that this belittles the power of what Jesus did on the cross, and it makes it seem like Jesus doesn't really have the power to save us forever.

TAKE THE DARE! — MY SECURITY PRAYER

This dare is a bit more difficult to take to an application level. Most of the dares end with a go-do-this challenge. This one is more like a go-know-this challenge! So have students personalize their responses to this truth by writing out a prayer to God.

Pass out a copy of **My Security Prayer** (Wildpage 11.2, page 84), and a pen or pencil to each student. Of course, if you used pens or pencils in a previous exercise, many will still have them. Some will, by now, have turned

You'll Need

ö copies of **My Security Prayer** Wildpage 11.2 (p. 84), pens or pencils for each student.

them into a destructive device and created a reason for yet another apology from you to the custodian.

Give them a bit of guidance about what they might want to consider writing. They could write about an area of their lives where they haven't been living like someone who belongs to Jesus (like one of the kids in the case studies).

Or they could write thanks to Jesus for knowing them and wanting them to belong to him.

Or both!

Ideally you'll have some mellow music you can play in the background while students complete this work. The music helps kids focus on what they're doing, rather than on the small noise distractions that are sure to occur (cough, sniff, sneeze, burp, fart).

After a few minutes, have students clump up in groups (unless your group is 10 kids or fewer; then just stay together). Ask if some would be willing to read their prayers during a time of prayer.

Give the groups a few minutes to pray. It would be best if you had an adult leader, or mature student you've assigned, in each group to wrap up the prayer time. Otherwise, you can wrap the prayer time from the front. ö

W i L D P A G E

Written For Today

The Bible was originally written by people and for people who totally understood shepherds and sheep—ideas most of us are not that familiar with today. Take a minute to rewrite this passage in your own words and in a way you think it might be written if the Bible were first written today and to teenagers. Don't use big important words—use your own words!

> **John 10:27-28**
> My sheep listen to my voice; I know them, and they follow me.
> I give them eternal life, and they shall never perish; no one can snatch them out of my hand.

✂ -

Written For Today

The Bible was originally written by people and for people who totally understood shepherds and sheep—ideas most of us are not that familiar with today. Take a minute to rewrite this passage in your own words and in a way you think it might be written if the Bible were first written today and to teenagers. Don't use big important words—use your own words!

> **John 10:27-28**
> My sheep listen to my voice; I know them, and they follow me.
> I give them eternal life, and they shall never perish; no one can snatch them out of my hand.

83

My Security Prayer

Write a prayer to God that either talks to him about an area of your life where you haven't been living as if you belong to Jesus (and how you need to change that), or to thank him for the security you have in him (and what it means to you):

- -

My Security Prayer

Write a prayer to God that either talks to him about an area of your life where you haven't been living as if you belong to Jesus (and how you need to change that), or to thank him for the security you have in him (and what it means to you):

Die

"I tell you the truth, unless a kernel of wheat falls to the ground and dies, it remains only a single seed. But if it dies, it produces many seeds. The man who loves his life will lose it, while the man who hates his life in this world will keep it for eternal life. Whoever serves me must follow me; and where I am, my servant also will be. My Father will honor the one who serves me."

John 12:24-26

GOALS

Students Will—

- Think about what is really important in their lives—not ice cream flavors, but life-and-death
- Talk about spiritual death, and what's at stake with their souls
- Join in prayers thanking God for offering us Real Life—and showing us how to die to self

Video clips: show a couple cheesy dying scenes from classic movies. A few suggestions:

Leo in *Titanic*
Tom Cruise in *Far and Away*
El Guapo in *The Three Amigos*
Darth Vader in *Return of the Jedi*

DYING DRAMAS

You'll Need

- ʘ nuthin' but participation, unless you want to give a candy prize to the "winning" team

Divide your students into teams: the size totally depends on the size of your group. If you have a small group (6 or fewer), don't divide. If your group is between 6 and 20 kids, use groups of 3 to 5. If your group is larger, then (duh!), use larger teams.

Ask each team to create a *very* short drama (about one minute long) that ends with one or more characters dying in a ridiculously cheesy way. Tell them to make sure the dying scene is *way* over-acted and silly. It would be great if you had an adult leader with each team to guide them.

After a few minutes, have the teams perform their scenes. Make sure you applaud wildly for each team and make this fun. Don't allow this to become a time when some kids feel dumb or rejected. If you use this as a competition, and told the teams they'll be judged solely on the creativity and cheesiness of the dying scene, award a small candy prize to the team that best meets those qualifications.

Option 2: Dying Moments

Ask a few volunteers to come to the front. They'll participate one at a time. Tell them you'll fire an imaginary gun at them, and their job is to make a huge display of dying—to really ham it up and drag it out. Make sure your group cheers them on and gives them lots of affirmation for participating.

Note: this option wouldn't be a good one if you're ministering in an urban setting or any place where shootings are a part of life. Instead of being fun, you'll be making sport of something very close to home.

You'll Need

- ʘ a few volunteers (students or adults) who are willing to ham it up

DEAD NO MORE PLAY-DOH

Divide your group into teams of, oh, whatever size you want! (Can you handle the pressure?)

Give each team a wad of Play-Doh or other modeling clay (you can make vatfuls of your own with the recipe in the sidebar). Tell them they're going to play a quick game of Play-Doh Pictionary. For each round a different person from each group will come up and get the word clue from you. Then they'll go back to their groups and model it with the clay until someone guesses what it is.

A few rules:

- They can't say or mouth anything!
- They're not allowed to spell things—make any letters or numbers—with the clay.
- Once someone in the group guesses the correct answer, they should shout out that their group finished.

Play each round like a new game, so teams always have an opportunity to win.

Don't tell them this yet: but all the clues are items that at one point appear to be dead, and then—come to find out—are not, either by waking up or by a sort of rebirth. You'll have them guess this later.

One more tip (I learned this through failure!): when you reveal the word clues to the players in each round, you either need to whisper it in each ear (or teams sitting near you will hear it), or you can show them the word on a piece of paper. But if you do the latter, I guarantee you that some of

your students will unknowingly mouth the word as they read it (it's a junior high twilight zone thing!). Make sure they don't do this, or, again, groups near you will see what they're saying and have an unfair advantage.

Here's the list:

Round 1: Bear
Round 2: Corn Kernel
Round 3: Caterpillar
Round 4: Acorn

After playing consider giving a candy prize to the group that got the most wins.

Then ask this way-important transitional question:

• **What do all these things—Bears, Corn Kernels, Caterpillars, and Acorns have in common?** You may have a perceptive kid who will get this right away, or you may have to offer a hint or two. Possible hints:

• **It's not something about how they look, but what they do. They all appear to be a certain way at one point or another** (this one's kind of a giveaway).

If one of your students shows amazing brilliance and pops off with the right answer—that these things all appear to be dead, and then come back to life (or, in fancier terms: they all have a dormant period)—toss that kid a candy bar or a six-pack (um, just kidding).

Now have students find in their Bibles this week's dare from Jesus: John 12:24-26. After reading it, lead a discussion with these questions:

• **How is a kernel of wheat like the clues in the game we just played?** (It falls to the ground and appears dead just like all the others.)

• **This is hard to understand: so, is Jesus saying that we have to physically die?** (No) **Then what do you think he means, that he wants us to die?** (Let your kids struggle with this for a bit

Homemade Clay Recipe

Ingredients:
1 cup all-purpose flour
1/2 cup salt
2 tsp. cream of tartar
1 cup water
1 tbsp. vegetable oil
Food coloring

In a saucepan, mix flour, salt, and cream of tartar over medium heat. Stir in water, oil, and food coloring (use your creativity for color).

Cook over medium heat, stirring constantly with a spatula until a ball forms (three to five minutes). When the dough becomes rubbery and pulls away from the sides of the saucepan, it's finished cooking. Knead the warm ball of fresh dough and store it in an airtight container at room temperature to keep it from drying out. It should last for months.

if they're not sure of the answer—don't come to their rescue too quickly. But at some point, make sure they understand what Jesus is talking about: that we need to surrender—to give ourselves up—in order to really experience life.)

• How about that part where Jesus says we should hate this world—what do you think that means? (Jesus is talking about priorities: if we love stuff in this world more than we love him, then we've got it all backwards.)

• So what to you think Jesus is daring us to do? (Let our own selfishness and control die, and give Jesus control of our lives—completely.)

Play-Doh-less option:

If you're a wimp and don't want to go get some Play-Doh, or if you're preparing this lesson 6 minutes before your group meets, you can always play the exact same game in two other ways:

As "win, loose or draw"—giving each team paper and pen and having them draw their clues (no letters or symbols, of course).

Or as traditional charades, with kids acting out the clues. I'd like to see how your kids act out "acorn!"

MINI-TALK

Explain briefly (like, in 3 minutes) what it means to die spiritually. This is extremely abstract, and you'll need to use simple concrete terms and concepts—especially if your group has 6th graders in it. Many of your students aren't very good at abstract thinking, and the concept of dying spiritually could easily fly in one ear and right out the other side, sounding like a nice churchy term (non-lodged right alongside "you need to be washed in the blood of the Lamb").

Help students understand that this dying stuff is a "once

You'll Need

ʚ nothing, really, but an overhead or whiteboard would help

and every day" thing. In other words, there comes a time when each of us chooses to give control of our lives to God and become Jesus followers. Some people call this "becoming a Christian." It's that moment when you choose to die, in a sense, to give up on running your own life and toss the reins to Jesus.

But there's a second kind of dying. And that comes every day: choosing again and again and again to be a Jesus follower. Explain that we all love to take the control back from God. And it's in this daily, or ongoing, dying to ourselves and our own desires that we get closer and closer to God.

Don't forget to talk about motivation. The *reason* Jesus wants us to take this dare isn't to mess up our lives! Go back to the *dare* verse—the reason is to give us life! This dying stuff produces *real* life!

Tip on terminology: I try to stay away from using the word "Christian" very often in explanation. Yup, it's a solid word with lots of good history (and some bad history!) And I'm not some freaky liberal who wants to remove Christ from Christmas (back off!) I've just experienced kids having lots of confusion over that term (not just kids—people in general), because it's evolved in its meaning to being something other than "Christ follower." So, I prefer to use terms like "Jesus follower," "Christ follower."

Feels Like i'm Dyin'

Lead an application-oriented discussion using the three case studies found on **Feels Like I'm Dyin'** (at the end of this lesson). A great way to present these is to choose three students (two girls and a boy) to read the monologues. It will make them more real for your students if they get to hear them read in the voice of a young teen. It would be best if you chose kids ahead of time who can read well. Give them the sheet so they can read it through on their own a few times.

You'll Need

ʚ either a few volunteers to read the monologues on the **Feels Like I'm Dyin'** sheet (p. 89) at the end of this lesson, or copies of the same sheet to hand out to everyone

You can always just copy the sheet and use it as a handout if you'd prefer, reading through the stories together.

Either way, spend some time after each monologue prodding your students to process the issue and offer suggestions. Depending on the maturity of your group, their comfort level with discussion, the tide level, and who knows what else (who can predict what will happen in junior high ministry?), this could be a powerful time of group processing. Or it could totally bomb!

Some thoughts for you, as you discuss these case studies:

- **Chelsea:** Dying to yourself, as Jesus dares us, doesn't mean we have to run toward the stuff we'd least like to do with our lives. It *does* mean we give God ultimate control of that decision. We stay open to whatever God leads us to. Maybe God *does* want Chelsea to be a doctor. Maybe God would want her to be a missionary doctor (be careful not to give kids the idea that being a missionary doctor means following God, and being a "regular" doctor doesn't.) Maybe God wants her to be something else altogether. The point is: if Chelsea "dies" on this subject, she'll give God control of her future.

- **Nate:** We're walking a fine balance here between offering kids real solutions and being overly simplistic (this is always a tension in junior high ministry). The key to Nate's story is that he's trying to fix himself—and that's not possible. This is where "dying" comes in: Nate needs to come to Jesus as he is and give up control of this area of his life. There's that tension—this can be a simplistic answer ("God will fix you in a jiffy!"). Focus more on the process than on a quick fix.

- **Lauren:** Again, this is about control. Lauren is trying to fix her parents. Maybe God *does* want to use Lauren to bring her parents back together. The point isn't what Lauren *does* or *doesn't do*. The point is the attitude of Lauren's heart—she's not giving control of her life to God in this area. If she "dies" in this area, she might still plan family outings and such, but her trust—for the care of her life and the care of her parents—will be in God, not in herself.

TIME TO DIE!

Before your group meets, make copies of **Time to Die!** (Wildpage 12.1, page 90) and cut them in half (across the dotted line, silly—cutting them lengthwise will make this really tough for your kids!).

Pass out the half-sheet copies and pens or pencils, to your students. Tell them they're about to do a very personal thing, and you don't want them to look at each other's papers or talk. If you have the space, it would be great if kids could spread out a bit to be less distracted by others.

Ask them to take about five minutes (it might take a bit longer than this, but some kids will be bouncing off the walls after a couple minutes of silence) to complete the three dares on the sheet. If possible play some fairly quiet background music while they're doing this: it decreases distractions.

After several minutes, pull your kids back together. You can wrap this up a couple ways. Ideally, you'd send your kids to small groups (if you're not using small groups, what are you thinking?) and give them a chance to talk about what they've written. Or, stay in a large group, and ask if a few students will read what they've written. You should model this by sharing an example of your own—and remember: your level of vulnerability will set the tone for how willing kids are to share (within limits: don't say, "I've been lusting over someone in this group!").

Either way, make sure you close your time in prayer, thanking God for wanting to give us real life, and asking God for courage to give him control.

Feels Like I'm Dyin'

Chelsea
Okay, I think I understand the idea of dying for God. But I'm having a hard time figuring out how it should affect my life. Take this example. Yesterday my mom was talking to me about what I want to do with my life—like, when I grow up. And she was pushing me to think about things like being a doctor, because I'm really good in science. And I said, "I don't know, Mom, maybe I should be a missionary or something—you know, totally give it up to God." She said, "Chelsea, you don't have to pretend that you don't have a brilliant brain to follow God." I thought that was a pretty mean slam on missionaries—like they couldn't do anything else and *had* to become a missionary or something. Anyhow, what do you think this idea of "dying" has to do with my life goal to be a scientist or doctor or something?

❂❂❂❂❂❂❂❂❂❂❂❂❂❂❂❂❂❂❂❂❂❂❂❂❂❂❂❂

Nate
Here's the deal: I've been really struggling with a certain sin for a while now. I'm too embarrassed about it to tell you what it is. But I feel guilty about it all the time. I've prayed about it like crazy. And this past summer at camp I made a big decision to unplug my computer—oh, that had something to do with the sin. Anyhow, I just went right back to it. I keep saying to myself, "I can fix this! I can stop! I can make myself clean for God!" But all my effort seems like a waste, 'cause I just keep doing it. Do you think this "dying to myself" stuff has anything to do with my problem? Do you have any advice for me?

❂❂❂❂❂❂❂❂❂❂❂❂❂❂❂❂❂❂❂❂❂❂❂❂❂❂❂❂

Lauren
My life stinks right now. My parents have been fighting like crazy, and a few months ago they started talking about getting a divorce. They're taking forever to decide, so I've been working like crazy to do everything I can to keep them together. I'm always pointing out my dad's good qualities to my mom. And I'm always making suggestions to my dad about ways he can be nice to my mom. I plan nice little family outings and dinners. Because I just feel like there's got to be a way I can fix this mess. In fact, I've been feeling like a total failure 'cause things haven't been getting any better. Okay, so God says I'm supposed to die. It already feels like I am! What does that have to do with my problem?

Time to Die!
Take these dares in this order:

Spend a minute praying, asking God to show you an area of your life
where you need to "die"—to give control to him.

Write one or two areas of your life where some death might lead to life:

Write a prayer to God and ask him to take control of this area of your life.

• •

Time to Die!
Take these dares in this order:

Spend a minute praying, asking God to show you an area of your life
where you need to "die"—to give control to him.

Write one or two areas of your life where some death might lead to life:

Write a prayer to God and ask him to take control of this area of your life.

Resources from Youth Specialties
www.youthspecialties.com

Ideas Library
Ideas Library on CD-ROM 2.0
Administration, Publicity, & Fundraising
Camps, Retreats, Missions, & Service Ideas
Creative Meetings, Bible Lessons, & Worship Ideas
Crowd Breakers & Mixers
Discussion & Lesson Starters
Discussion & Lesson Starters 2
Drama, Skits, & Sketches
Drama, Skits, & Sketches 2
Drama, Skits, & Sketches 3
Games
Games 2
Games 3
Holiday Ideas
Special Events

Bible Curricula
Backstage Pass to the Bible Kit
Creative Bible Lessons from the Old Testament
Creative Bible Lessons in 1 & 2 Corinthians
Creative Bible Lessons in Galatians and Philippians
Creative Bible Lessons in John
Creative Bible Lessons in Romans
Creative Bible Lessons on the Life of Christ
Creative Bible Lessons on the Prophets
Creative Bible Lessons in Psalms
Wild Truth Bible Lessons
Wild Truth Bible Lessons 2
Wild Truth Bible Lessons—Pictures of God
Wild Truth Bible Lessons—Pictures of God 2
Wild Truth Bible Lessons—Dares from Jesus

Topical Curricula
Creative Junior High Programs from A to Z, Vol. 1 (A-M)
Creative Junior High Programs from A to Z, Vol. 2 (N-Z)
Girls: 10 Gutsy, God-Centered Sessions on Issues That Matter to Girls
Guys: 10 Fearless, Faith-Focused Sessions on Issues That Matter to Guys
Good Sex
The Justice Mission
Live the Life! Student Evangelism Training Kit
The Next Level Youth Leader's Kit
Roaring Lambs
So What Am I Gonna Do with My Life?

Topical Curricula (cont)
Student Leadership Training Manual
Student Underground
Talking the Walk
What Would Jesus Do? Youth Leader's Kit
Wild Truth Bible Lessons
Wild Truth Bible Lessons 2
Wild Truth Bible Lessons—Pictures of God
Wild Truth Bible Lessons—Pictures of God 2
Wild Truth Bible Lessons—Dares from Jesus

Discussion Starters
Discussion & Lesson Starters (Ideas Library)
Discussion & Lesson Starters 2 (Ideas Library)
EdgeTV
Every Picture Tells a Story
Get 'Em Talking
Keep 'Em Talking!
Good Sex Drama
Have You Ever...?
Name Your Favorite
Unfinished Sentences
What If...?
Would You Rather...?
High School TalkSheets—Updated!
More High School TalkSheets—Updated!
High School TalkSheets from Psalms and Proverbs—Updated!
Junior High-Middle School TalkSheets—Updated!
More Junior High-Middle School TalkSheets—Updated!
Junior High-Middle School TalkSheets from Psalms and Proverbs—Updated!
Real Kids Ultimate Discussion-Starting Videos:
      Castaways
      Growing Up Fast
      Hardship & Healing
      Quick Takes
      Survivors
      Word on the Street
Small Group Qs

Drama Resources
Drama, Skits, & Sketches (Ideas Library)
Drama, Skits, & Sketches 2 (Ideas Library)
Drama, Skits, & Sketches 3 (Ideas Library)
Dramatic Pauses
Good Sex Drama
Spontaneous Melodramas
Spontaneous Melodramas 2
Super Sketches for Youth Ministry

Game Resources

Games (Ideas Library)
Games 2 (Ideas Library)
Games 3 (Ideas Library)
Junior High Game Nights
More Junior High Game Nights
Play It!
Screen Play CD-ROM

Additional Programming Resources
(also see Discussion Starters)

The Book of Uncommon Prayers
Camps, Retreats, Missions, & Service Ideas (Ideas Library)
Creative Meetings, Bible Lessons, & Worship Ideas (Ideas Library)
Crowd Breakers & Mixers (Ideas Library)
Everyday Object Lessons
Great Fundraising Ideas for Youth Groups
More Great Fundraising Ideas for Youth Groups
Great Retreats for Youth Groups
Great Talk Outlines for Youth Ministry
Holiday Ideas (Ideas Library)
Incredible Questionnaires for Youth Ministry
Kickstarters
Memory Makers
Special Events (Ideas Library)
Videos That Teach
Videos That Teach 2
Worship Services for Youth Groups

Quick Question Books

Have You Ever...?
Name Your Favorite
Unfinished Sentences
What If...?
Would You Rather...?

Digital Resources

Clip Art Library Version 2.0 (CD-ROM)
Great Talk Outlines for Youth Ministry
Hot Illustrations CD-ROM
Ideas Library on CD-ROM 2.0
Screen Play
Youth Ministry Management Tools

Videos & Video Curricula

Dynamic Communicators Workshop

EdgeTV

The Justice Mission

Live the Life! Student Evangelism Training Kit

Make 'Em Laugh!

Purpose-Driven® Youth Ministry Training Kit

Real Kids Ultimate Discussion-Starting Videos:

> Castaways
>
> Growing Up Fast
>
> Hardship & Healing
>
> Quick Takes
>
> Survivors
>
> Word on the Street

Student Underground

Understanding Your Teenager Video Curriculum

Youth Ministry Outside the Lines

Especially for Junior High

Creative Junior High Programs from A to Z, Vol. 1 (A-M)

Creative Junior High Programs from A to Z, Vol. 2 (N-Z)

Junior High Game Nights

More Junior High Game Nights

Junior High-Middle School TalkSheets—Updated!

More Junior High-Middle School TalkSheets—Updated!

Junior High-Middle School TalkSheets from Psalms and Proverbs—Updated!

Wild Truth Journal for Junior Highers

Wild Truth Bible Lessons

Wild Truth Bible Lessons 2

Wild Truth Journal—Pictures of God

Wild Truth Bible Lessons—Pictures of God

Wild Truth Bible Lessons—Dares from Jesus

Wild Truth Journal—Dares from Jesus

Student Resources

Backstage Pass to the Bible: An All-Access Tour of the New Testament

Backstage Pass to the Bible: An All-Access Tour of the Old Testament

Grow for It! Journal through the Scriptures

So What Am I Gonna Do with My Life?

Spiritual Challenge Journal: The Next Level

Teen Devotional Bible

What (Almost) Nobody Will Tell You about Sex

What Would Jesus Do? Spiritual Challenge Journal

Clip Art

Youth Group Activities (print)
Clip Art Library Version 2.0 (CD-ROM)

Professional Resources

Administration, Publicity, & Fundraising (Ideas Library)
Dynamic Communicators Workshop
Great Talk Outlines for Youth Ministry
Help! I'm a Junior High Youth Worker!
Help! I'm a Small Church Youth Worker!
Help! I'm a Small-Group Leader!
Help! I'm a Sunday School Teacher!
Help! I'm an Urban Youth Worker!
Help! I'm a Volunteer Youth Worker!
Hot Illustrations for Youth Talks
More Hot Illustrations for Youth Talks
Still More Hot Illustrations for Youth Talks
Hot Illustrations for Youth Talks 4
How to Expand Your Youth Ministry
How to Speak to Youth...and Keep Them Awake at the Same Time
Junior High Ministry (Updated & Expanded)
Just Shoot Me
Make 'Em Laugh!
The Ministry of Nurture
Postmodern Youth Ministry
Purpose-Driven® Youth Ministry
Purpose-Driven® Youth Ministry Training Kit
So That's Why I Keep Doing This!
Teaching the Bible Creatively
Your First Two Years in Youth Ministry
A Youth Ministry Crash Course
Youth Ministry Management Tools
The Youth Worker's Handbook to Family Ministry

Academic Resources

Four Views of Youth Ministry & the Church
Starting Right
Youth Ministry That Transforms